MW00826287

ARCHAEOLOGY OF JESUS' NAZARETH

ARCHAEOLOGY OF JESUS' NAZARETH

KEN DARK

OXFORD
UNIVERSITY PRESS

OXFORD
UNIVERSITY PRESS

Great Clarendon Street, Oxford, OX2 6DP,
United Kingdom

Oxford University Press is a department of the University of Oxford.
It furthers the University's objective of excellence in research, scholarship,
and education by publishing worldwide. Oxford is a registered trade mark of
Oxford University Press in the UK and in certain other countries

First Edition published in 2023

Impression: 1

Published in the United States of America by Oxford University Press
198 Madison Avenue, New York, NY 10016, United States of America

British Library Cataloguing in Publication Data
Data available

Library of Congress Control Number: 2022941521

ISBN 978–0–19–286539–7

DOI: 10.1093/oso/9780192865397.001.0001

Printed and bound by
CPI Group (UK) Ltd, Croydon, CR0 4YY

Preface: Purpose, Sources, and References

Nazareth—today a small city in the Galilee region of northern Israel—is most famous, of course, for being where the Gospels say that Jesus Christ grew up and lived in the early first century AD. It might be imagined that this would have attracted many archaeologists to work in Nazareth. But, in fact, Nazareth was largely neglected by archaeologists between the early 1970s and the start of my own work on its archaeology in 2004.

This book is written to explain what, after eighteen years of research, I think we know, or can reasonably figure out, about early first-century Nazareth and its immediate vicinity. Almost all of the information we have about this subject, outside of the Gospels, is from archaeology, hence the book's title.

It is more specifically designed to answer the most frequent questions about my work on Nazareth that I have been asked by people who aren't archaeologists. It is also intended to clear up some misunderstandings about it, deriving mostly from media reports.

As such, although it contains new interpretations which may be of interest to professional archaeologists, historians, and experts in biblical studies, the primary purpose of this book is to explain, to readers other than archaeologists, research that has so far been published mainly in an academic manner. Hopefully, this will lead to a new understanding of what archaeology really shows us about early first-century Nazareth ('Jesus' Nazareth').

For that reason, the present book brings together information from three of my earlier academic publications. Chapter 2 is based on my 2020 book *Roman-period and Byzantine Nazareth and its Hinterland*, and the remainder is based on my book *The Sisters of Nazareth Convent*, published the following year, and my 2016 Henry Myers Lecture to the Royal Anthropological Institute, 'Returning to the Caves of Mystery'. This was also published in 2020 in the academic archaeology journal *Strata*.

My two earlier books cover a much wider time span than the present work. Here only evidence concerning the first century AD—or, although later, evidence that is of significance to understanding first-century Nazareth—is discussed. Anyone interested in Byzantine—that is, fifth- to seventh-century AD—or later Nazareth and its immediately surrounding landscape may consult those two books.

It is an indication of how little archaeological attention has been paid to Nazareth since the fieldwork on which my two earlier books were based that there are only five more recent publications, and five brief online reports of Israel Antiquities Authority fieldwork—given in the References section—relevant to this book.

Three of the publications establish that limestone vessels—like pottery cups and other containers, but made out of stone—were manufactured for longer in the Roman period than previously thought. These don't affect the arguments and interpretation in my earlier books or those given here.

The very interesting recent paper on the 'Nazareth Inscription' shows that I and others were almost certainly right in supposing that it has nothing to do with Nazareth. It is discussed at the appropriate point in Chapter 2.

David Fiensy's book, written from the perspective of a biblical scholar, is less directly relevant to Nazareth but includes a few examples drawn from Nazareth's archaeology (for example, the photo—Figure 4.7—on page 96). It offers an interesting context into which to put the interpretations discussed in Chapter 6 here, and is worth reading for anyone seeking information about the first-century Holy Land.

The References section includes full references to my three earlier publications and these more recent works. It also contains books which help to put my own work in the context of other studies of Nazareth's archaeology and that of the region of Galilee (also called 'the Galilee') in which Nazareth is situated.

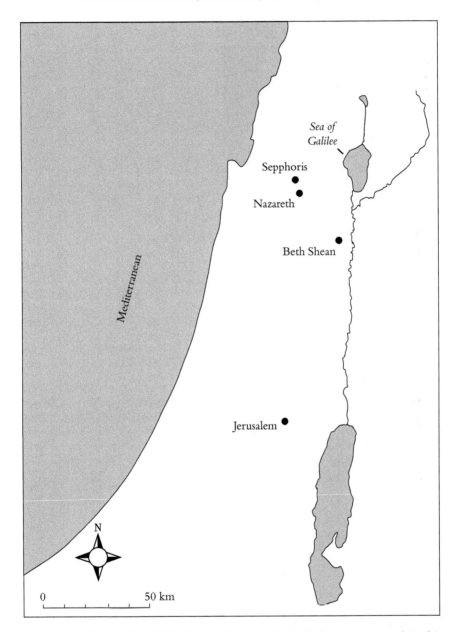

Figure o.1. Map of the Holy Land, with the principal places mentioned in this book indicated. From *The Sisters of Nazareth convent. A Roman-period, Byzantine and Crusader site in central Nazareth*, 1st ed., by Ken Dark, copyright 2021 by Imprint; reproduced by permission of Taylor & Francis Group.

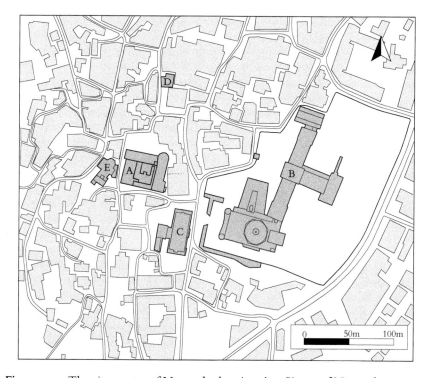

Figure 0.2. The city centre of Nazareth, showing: A = Sisters of Nazareth convent; B = Church of the Annunciation complex; C = Casa Nova hostel; D = Synagogue Church; E = Anglican church. Drawn by Ifan Edwards for the Nazareth Archaeological Project, based on the city of Nazareth map of the Israel National Survey. From *The Sisters of Nazareth convent. A Roman-period, Byzantine and Crusader site in central Nazareth*, 1st ed., by Ken Dark, copyright 2021 by Imprint. Reproduced by permission of Taylor & Francis Group.

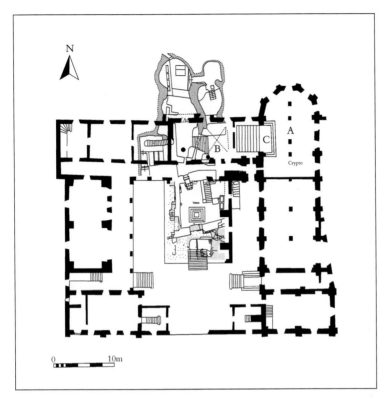

Figure o.3. Convent plan and location of its 'Cellar'. A = convent chapel; B = convent museum; C = modern stairway to Cellar. Drawn by Ifan Edwards for the Nazareth Archaeological Project. From *The Sisters of Nazareth convent. A Roman-period, Byzantine and Crusader site in central Nazareth*, 1st ed., by Ken Dark, copyright 2021 by Imprint; reproduced by permission of Taylor & Francis Group.

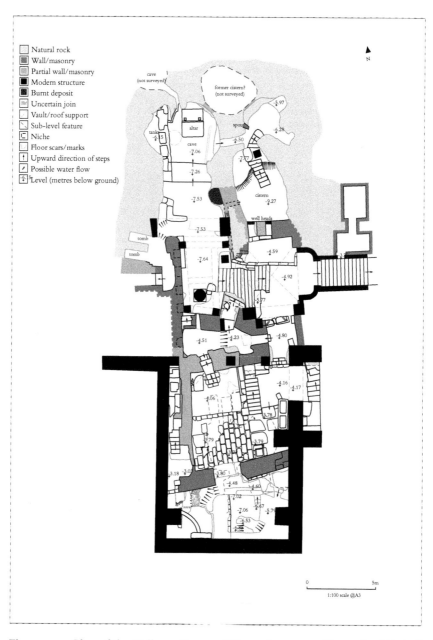

Figure 0.4. Plan of the Cellar at Sisters of Nazareth convent. Drawn by Mitchell Pollington for the Nazareth Archaeological Project. From *The Sisters of Nazareth convent. A Roman-period, Byzantine and Crusader site in central Nazareth*, 1st ed., by Ken Dark, copyright 2021 by Imprint; reproduced by permission of Taylor & Francis Group.

Acknowledgements

My work in, and near, Nazareth was only possible with permission and help of the Israel Antiquities Authority (IAA). Thanks are also, of course, due to the Sisters of Nazareth for permission to work at the convent and for all their help, especially the convent superior in 2006, Sister Margherita, and her successor, Sister Stefania.

Ifan Edwards was responsible for most of the drawings in this book, assisted in the field by Helen Robertson. Mitchell Pollington made the detailed plans of the Sisters of Nazareth 'Cellar' and the quarry reproduced here.

I am also, of course, grateful for the help provided in Nazareth by other members of the British survey team, who are individually acknowledged in my two previous books, as are the many friends and colleagues who have discussed the archaeology of Nazareth with me. My fieldwork discussed here was funded by the Palestine Exploration Fund and the Late Antiquity Research Group, both secular, non-political, British academic archaeological organizations.

Contents

List of Figures

(Scales in all the photographs are in 10 centimetre divisions.)

Terminology and Timescales

In accordance with the normal conventions of British—and most other European—studies of Roman archaeology, dating is given using the AD/BC system, rather than the CE/BCE system widely used in American and Israeli archaeology. If you prefer the CE/BCE system, it is easy to convert these dates, because 1 CE is equivalent to AD 1; 1 BCE to 1 BC. For convenience, the region today encompassed within modern Israel and the Palestinian territories is called here 'the Holy Land'.

The main historical periods with which this book is concerned are the Hellenistic period, from the fourth century BC until the Roman conquest, the Roman period—which in Galilee is from the late first century BC until the end of the fourth century AD—and the Byzantine period, which in this region dates from the fifth century AD until the seventh century. The Byzantine period was interrupted near its end by a Persian invasion in the early seventh century, and followed by the Muslim conquest later in the seventh century. Muslim control of Nazareth ceased when the European Crusaders took the city in 1099. The Crusaders lost Nazareth in 1187, but effective Crusader control of the town was restored between 1250 and 1263, after which it again came under Muslim control.

It will also be convenient to divide the Roman period into two. The Early Roman period is considered here to last until the mid-third century; the Late Roman period, to comprise the later third century until the end of the fourth century. In the early fourth century, the Roman Empire's policy towards Christianity dramatically shifted from a mixture of persecution and indifference to active support.

A few other archaeological terms may benefit from clarification: 'archaeological fieldwork'—often just 'fieldwork' for short—is conventionally used as the term for scientific excavation, archaeological survey, or both. 'Section' is used in archaeology for a vertical face of soil, such as that visible at the edges of a scientific excavation; 'elevation' is used for the vertical face of a wall. Likewise, a 'plan' is a horizontal map of a surface exposed by archaeological excavation or recorded by survey. Fragments of pottery are called 'sherds'; fragments of glass termed 'shards'.

The concept of stratigraphy is fundamental to dating archaeological excavations. According to this concept, any layer (a layer being an approximately horizontal deposit of soil) on top of another must be later than that below it. Likewise, a feature (a cut down into the surface of a layer, or of the underlying natural rock, or alternatively something, such as a wall, built up from the surface of a layer) must be later than any layer or other feature which it cuts into or overlies. This concept enables the archaeologist to understand the sequence in which layers and features developed, and thereby understand the sequence of human activity on a site.

Dating archaeological layers and features depends on two other concepts. The stratigraphical law of *terminus post quem* states that a layer must be the same date or later than the latest 'sealed' object which is found in it. 'Sealed' in this sense means that the object cannot be shown to have got into the layer later, pushed down through animal burrows or plant roots, for example. A layer containing a sealed sherd of Roman pottery, therefore, must date from the Roman period or later.

This has to be combined with another stratigraphical law, the law of *terminus ante quem*. This states that if the date of a layer or feature is absolutely known—for example, due to an inscription giving a calendar date or due to distinctive characteristics of its construction—then any layer or feature below it, or cut by it, must be that date or earlier. Consequently, if a wall certainly dates to the first century, because it incorporates an inscription giving it that date or because of its constructional style, any layer or feature below it or cut by it must be first century or earlier.

Of course, sometimes in archaeological work we can use laboratory science to provide other forms of dating—such as radiocarbon dates—but these methods, as we shall see, have played very little role in the archaeology of first-century Nazareth.

It might be useful to explain a few other terms used in this book which may be unfamiliar to some readers. Archaeology, like most academic disciplines, uses a lot of specialized language—what might be called 'technical terms'. Overall, I have avoided these when something can be explained in ordinary English.

For example, the characteristic rock-cut storage pits found in Roman-period Nazareth, with their pear-shaped profiles, are termed here 'storage pits' or 'rock-cut storage pits', rather than 'silos' or 'piriform silos'—which they are called in most of the academic descriptions of Nazareth's archaeology.

Of course, it is sometimes necessary to describe something of which the meaning—although it isn't specific to archaeology—might be unfamiliar to some readers, but well known to others. In this context, it may be useful to consider the following terms.

When describing a church, it is conventional to call the congregational space, where most people stand or sit during worship, the 'nave', and the curved end of the church, where the altar is, the 'apse'.

The ceremonies that take place during Christian worship are called the 'liturgy', and those parts of the church used especially in them—for example, the altar—are, therefore, sometimes described as the church's 'liturgical fittings'. They are also called 'church furniture' in some publications, but that term is so confusing—to me its sounds like the pews where people sit—that it isn't used here. Likewise, a 'cathedral' is the bishop's principal church, usually larger than all the others in an urban centre. Following colloquial English usage, one can call any urban place with a cathedral a city.

When describing farming practices in Galilee, an 'olive press' is an installation for the production of olive oil by crushing olives, and a 'wine press' the equivalent for producing wine by crushing grapes. An 'agricultural terrace' is a piece of ground on a slope, such as a hillside, made approximately flat for farming purposes.

Other frequently used terms specific to the archaeology of Nazareth:

Wall 1—the main north–south rock-cut wall of Structure 1 at the Sisters of Nazareth site and its continuation to form the south wall of the Chambre Obscure.

Wall 2—the built wall to the east of Wall 1.

Chambre Obscure—the small rock-cut room immediately north of Wall 1.

Structure 1—the partly rock-cut room formed by Wall 1 and, perhaps, the original version of Wall 2, and the Chambre Obscure.

M4—the large medieval built wall running east–west across the Cellar at the Sisters of Nazareth site, slightly curving northward to support a vaulted ceiling once covering the areas between Wall 1 and Wall 2.

Nahal Zippori—the broad valley between Nazareth and the Roman town of Sepphoris to its north.

Church of the Nutrition—a modern name for the church built by the Byzantines where they believed the house in which Jesus was brought up by Mary and Joseph had once stood.

Structure of the Book

It may help at this point to outline the structure of the book. Chapter 1 tells the story of how I came to be involved in the archaeology of Nazareth. Chapter 2 describes what is known about the archaeology of first-century Nazareth in general.

Chapters 3 to 5 concern the fascinating Sisters of Nazareth site, the focus of my own work in the centre of the modern city. This is the site with the famous 'House of Jesus'—probably a genuine first-century domestic structure (that is, what might be called a 'house')—claimed since the nineteenth century to be the place where Jesus was brought up by Mary and Joseph.

Chapter 3 discusses the excavations by nineteenth-century nuns at the site—one of the earliest examples worldwide of an archaeological excavation being initiated, undertaken, and directed by women. Then Chapter 4 recounts the lifelong, but unfulfilled, quest of a Catholic priest to discover the truth about the site.

Chapter 5 describes my own study of the Sisters of Nazareth site, which examined and interpreted it according to the latest archaeological methods and concepts. This gets as close as we can at present to knowing what was actually found at the site.

Finally, Chapter 6 brings all of this together to consider what we really know about first-century Nazareth as a place, what it was like to live there, and where the Sisters of Nazareth site fits in. The book ends by briefly discussing what all this might mean for understanding the Gospels.

I

An accidental biblical
archaeologist?

The fact is that I didn't come to Nazareth to search for Jesus' village. Nor was I in Nazareth as a 'biblical archaeologist', studying what archaeological research can tell us about the Bible. That subdiscipline barely exists in twenty-first-century Britain.

Instead, I came to Nazareth to examine archaeological evidence for its role as a Byzantine pilgrimage centre. Discovering new evidence about the first-century settlement during that work led me to reconsider the archaeology of first-century Nazareth as a whole. This is how it happened.

I was a university-based professional archaeologist, specializing in the first millennium AD in Europe and the Middle East. Much of my work had been on what might be called secular (non-religious) topics—especially the collapse of the Roman Empire, the kingdoms which replaced it in Western Europe, and its continuation in the eastern Mediterranean as the Byzantine state. An important motivation of my research on this subject was trying to understand the dynamics of states and societies over very long periods of time.

That research led me to do archaeological work in the centre of Istanbul, which—as the city of Constantinople—had been the capital of the Byzantine Empire. In 2004, having finished seven years of archaeological work there, I was looking for a contrasting rural location to continue my research on the Roman and Byzantine archaeology of the Middle East. What I wanted to do next was to examine the rise of a Late Roman—fourth-century AD—Christian pilgrimage centre against the background of its Roman landscape. This would feed into wider debates about the role of Christianity in the transformation of the Roman Empire into the medieval world.

There were many questions to answer, and the answers could have implications beyond any single place. When a pilgrimage centre was established, did local people get richer? Was the landscape more multicultural after the pilgrims arrived? How many of the local population actually converted to Christianity?

That is, to what extent did the emergence of Late Roman pilgrimage centres cause a major shift in the way people lived? Or was it just another chapter in a long story of gradual transition from the Roman to post-Roman world?

What I needed to look at was a place which became a Christian pilgrimage site in the Late Roman period and then flourished in the Early Byzantine period, the fifth to seventh centuries. Then it would be possible to use conventional archaeological methods to investigate the site itself and its surrounding landscape to assess its origins and impact.

If possible, this would be based on archaeological survey, which is cheaper, easier to set up, and for which it is usually easier to get permission, than digging holes. Today, archaeological survey methods can answer a lot of the questions that only excavation could address in earlier generations.

More specifically, it might be possible to identify a pattern of Roman-period farms and villages, and trace how they changed over time, looking for indicators of wealth and cultural and religious identity. Other studies had found such indicators elsewhere, so this seemed fairly straightforward as an archaeological project. The question was, where to do it?

Initial enquiries produced various possibilities in Egypt, Greece, and Syria. All were attractive in different ways, but when the opportunity came up to conduct my project in Israel, I knew that this would be the best option. Christianity, of course, began there, and it was there also that the earliest Christian pilgrimage centres were located.

In the course of discussion with the archaeological authorities in Israel, they sent a long list of possible areas for which permission might be given. When I saw that one of these was 'Nazareth', that was it—my project was going to be on Nazareth. After all, where better to look at the long-term consequences of a place becoming a Christian pilgrimage site than Jesus' 'home town'?

After a certain amount of the usual bureaucratic form-filling and other official processes, fortunately permission was given to begin work in and around Nazareth the same year. This led to two years of identifying and mapping surface features and fieldwalking. The latter is literally systematically walking across ploughed fields, recording the pieces of broken pottery (sherds) and other objects exposed by farming, construction, and even natural erosion.

Elsewhere in what was once the Roman Empire, fieldwalking has proved remarkably effective at recognizing farms or villages across whole landscapes. Nahal Zippori, the valley between modern Nazareth and the excavated ruins of the Roman town of Sepphoris 6 kilometres to its north, is perfect for this technique: large, open fields easily accessed by modern roads and tracks. (See Figures 1.1 and 1.2.) Almost all the fields were either ploughed or used for olive trees, with the soil between the trees exposed or even ploughed. They could be surveyed quickly by a small team.

The land falls sharply to the south of the modern city of Nazareth. So the valley to its north and the area beneath the modern city were probably where the agricultural land of ancient Nazareth was located.

Fieldwalking in the valley was a hot and dusty business. The landscape is hilly, rocky, and exposed—and we were working in the full heat of the

Figure 1.1. The valley between Nazareth and Sepphoris, looking north. Photo: Ken Dark.

Figure 1.2. The valley between Nazareth and Sepphoris, looking east. Photo: Ken Dark.

Middle Eastern summer. The only shelter from the sun was in the olive plantations.

This soon produced exciting new information. The valley turned out to be full of previously undiscovered Roman-period sites. There were at least twenty-three in a single 5 by 3 kilometre strip. The reason that they had been missed by previous archaeologists was probably that most were visible on the surface of the ground only as concentrations of pottery sherds in the fields. A few also had evidence of small-scale quarrying of the local limestone—unfinished building blocks could still be seen partly cut out. (See Figure 1.3.)

Judging from the pottery and other ancient objects found on the surface, these were Roman-period farms and very small villages, with no evidence of great wealth or specialized functions.

It is easy to explain why there were so many farms in the valley: the area around Nazareth is especially agriculturally fertile, with good, well-watered soils. Compared to most of the region there is high rainfall—it is said that the annual rainfall in Nazareth today is approximately the same as that in

Figure 1.3. Roman-period quarrying in the valley between Nazareth and Sepphoris showing cuts to extract blocks. Photo: Ken Dark.

London! Because of this, a wide range of crops can be grown, including the staples of the ancient Mediterranean diet: wheat, grapes, and olives.

Although these farms and villages probably belonged to Jewish communities, all farming the valley in a similar way, sites closer to Sepphoris had a different range of objects from those closer to Nazareth. (See Figure 1.4.) Of course, when we found these objects they were broken into pieces, but nevertheless they were easily identifiable.

Near Nazareth, these Roman-period settlements had only types of artefacts which are known to have been made by Jews. But on the Sepphoris side of the same valley the sites had a much wider range of artefacts, including those imported from non-Jewish communities.

There is an obvious explanation for this: communities closer to Nazareth—and, as we shall see later, those living in Nazareth—observed the Jewish purity laws of the time much more strictly than those living closer to Sepphoris.

Sepphoris had already been extensively excavated and found to have a similar range of artefacts to the newly discovered settlements on its side of

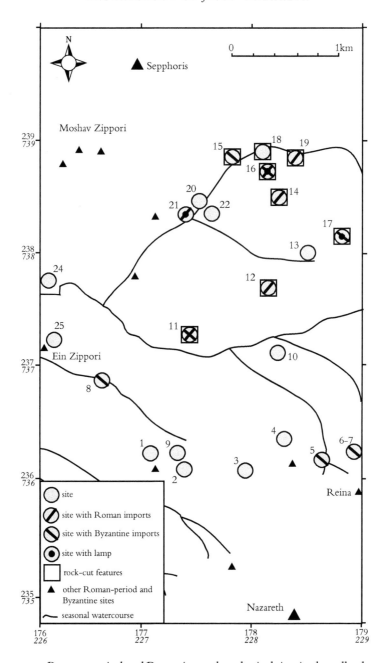

Figure 1.4. Roman-period and Byzantine archaeological sites in the valley between Nazareth and Sepphoris identified in the 2004–5 survey. From *Roman-period and Byzantine Nazareth and its hinterland*, 1st ed., by Ken Dark, copyright 2020 by Imprint; reproduced by permission of Taylor & Francis Group.

the valley. Also, the few earlier excavations in Nazareth have produced a similar range of objects to those found on its side of the valley.

Consequently, the survey provides evidence for something unique in the archaeology of the whole Roman Empire: a distinct border between adjacent communities accepting Roman provincial culture and those rejecting it, and an explanation for why that border existed.

In the Byzantine period—the fifth to seventh centuries—this border disappeared. Communities on both sides of the former dividing line used the same range of objects. These objects included imported pottery which would apparently have been unacceptable to groups close to Nazareth centuries before, because it was made by non-Jews. The cultural divide between communities on the two sides of the valley was over, but the question is, 'why'?

Perhaps there was a transformation in the religious attitudes of Jewish communities closer to Nazareth. Perhaps these communities became more liberal in their views and abandoned their previous reservations about imported goods. Alternatively, the emergence of the Christian pilgrimage centre at Nazareth may have led to the conversion of Jewish communities in its hinterland. These communities might, therefore, be expected to abandon the Jewish purity laws and, perhaps, more fully embrace Late Roman culture in general.

No similar transformation seems to have occurred in Sepphoris. In the Byzantine period the town had large Christian and Jewish communities living side by side. Indeed, excavated evidence shows both a large church and a synagogue there, both with multicoloured mosaic floors.

The quarry sites also showed an interesting pattern. (See Figures 1.5 and 1.6.) Some were on the Sepphoris side of the valley. This might be expected, because a large Roman town would have needed a lot of building stone. But some were nearer Nazareth, and, to judge from the pottery found at them, these quarries were used in the Roman period. If so, why did what was usually considered by archaeologists to have been a very small village—a 'hamlet'—have a group of quarries around it? Was it a quarry-workers' settlement? We will return to this question in Chapter 6.

Perhaps, then, the rise of Nazareth as a pilgrimage centre did have important consequences for the surrounding population. However, in the course of studying the valley, it became clear just how little was known about Late Roman and Byzantine Nazareth itself. The only major archaeological work had

Figure 1.5. Roman-period quarrying in the valley between Nazareth and Sepphoris. Photo: Ken Dark.

been in the 1960s and early 1970s, using methods which few archaeologists studying the Roman Empire would today employ.

What was needed next, therefore, was a new investigation of the Roman-period and Byzantine archaeology of Nazareth itself. Obviously, this was going to be difficult, because the little that was known of the archaeology of ancient Nazareth showed that it was in the centre of the modern city of the same name.

Nazareth today is a bustling town of about 60,000 people. It might be imagined that it would be a major tourist centre, but in fact most tourists in Nazareth in the first decade of the twenty-first century were visiting just for the day on coach trips. They usually went only to the Church of the Annunciation, the main—cathedral-size—church in the city centre, and to a few other places presented as of Christian interest.

It looked as if the only way to find out more about Roman-period or Byzantine Nazareth was going to be to dig. The problem was, where? The town is heavily built-up, with houses and shops crowded into narrow streets. There are very few open spaces other than within religious

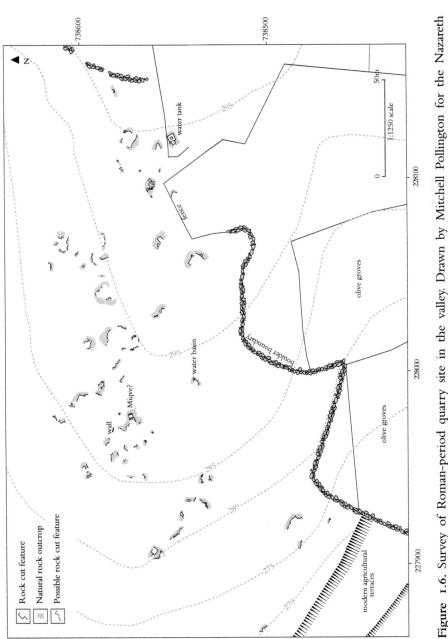

Figure 1.6. Survey of Roman-period quarry site in the valley. Drawn by Mitchell Pollington for the Nazareth Archaeological Project; from *Roman-period and Byzantine Nazareth and its hinterland*, 1st ed., by Ken Dark, copyright 2020 by Imprint; reproduced by permission of Taylor & Francis Group.

establishments—and they seemed unlikely to want an excavation in their gardens and courtyards.

This was when I decided to walk around every street in the town, looking for Roman or Byzantine stonework, or even walls, incorporated into later buildings or in their yards. My previous work in Istanbul had shown this technique to be a very useful way to identify the locations of Byzantine buildings in a modern city. I hoped that this might be the case in Nazareth also.

But a few days of this in Nazareth and the answer was apparent: there was no Roman or Byzantine stonework to be seen. Literally none.

Perplexed, I thought the only thing to do was to visit all the locations where archaeological publications said that things had been found during the little previous archaeological work in the city. Most of these were nineteenth-century finds, and their sites had been developed and altered beyond all recognition. Again, nothing was visible of these earlier discoveries.

There was only one thing left to do—visit the few ancient monuments in the town displayed for tourists and pilgrims. I made a list—a very short list—of what there was to see. This was little more than a tourist itinerary around Nazareth, but I hoped that it might offer some possibilities for further work.

As I worked my way down the list, the sites began to fall into two categories: those that were in or around churches and unavailable for study, and those which were medieval or later—much too late in date for my project.

For example, the 'Synagogue Church', said to be where the synagogue in Jesus' Nazareth stood, is a wholly medieval building. In fact, there is no evidence that a synagogue, or any other Roman-period public building for that matter, ever stood there.

Despondent, I returned to my hotel, a modern multistorey building on a hill in what was then called Nazaret 'Illit—upper Nazareth—outside the old town. You could see it from some parts of the city centre, contrasting with the nineteenth- and early twentieth-century architecture there.

After days of scouring the town there was no site that could be excavated, even if I could get official permission to do so. There was only one place left on my list: the Sisters of Nazareth convent.

Sitting in the hotel's European-style bar, I looked up the Sisters of Nazareth site in a tourist guidebook. (See Figure 1.7.) For my purpose, the entry for the convent was far from encouraging.

Figure 1.7. The Sisters of Nazareth convent seen from the street, showing the entrance. From *The Sisters of Nazareth convent. A Roman-period, Byzantine and Crusader site in central Nazareth*, 1st ed., by Ken Dark, copyright 2021 by Imprint; reproduced by permission of Taylor & Francis Group.

Figure 1.8. Tomb 1. The 'First-century Jewish tomb' which I had come to see on my first visit to the convent in 2005. Photo: Ken Dark.

It said that a 'first-century Jewish tomb' could be seen in the cellar of the French-speaking convent. But it could only be viewed with an appointment, to be made by telephoning the convent. (See Figure 1.8.)

I could imagine what would happen if I did get an appointment. A nun in a habit was going to lead me through the silent corridors to an old stairway. She would unlock a small under-stair door. I would peer into the blackness of the cellar, where a small part of a rock-cut tomb would be barely visible in the darkness, make polite noises about how interesting it was, thank her, and leave.

But I had nothing else left to do. So I asked the young woman at the hotel reception desk if she knew how to book a visit to the convent. She did and, what was more, she would be happy to phone them for me straight away.

I told her that the nuns might speak only French. She laughed and told me that she was a Catholic and had been to a French-speaking convent school. She was used to talking to nuns.

A few minutes later an appointment was booked at the Sisters of Nazareth convent for the next day. All I needed to do was go to the convent porter's lodge and someone would show me the tomb.

Next morning, it was off in a taxi to central Nazareth. The convent turned out to be up a side street just across from the Church of the Annunciation. The latter was one of the few places where much had previously been found from the Roman-period village, along with the remains of Byzantine and Crusader churches. The Church of the Annunciation site is discussed in the next chapter.

But from the outside the convent looked archaeologically unpromising. The plain façade obviously dated from the late nineteenth or early twentieth century, built in distinctive pale grey—almost white—stone. The double main gates were locked and entry was through a smaller door to one side. I rang the bell for attention and was let in by someone speaking in French. So far it all fitted with my expectations.

In the porter's lodge—just inside the gates, like those in Oxford or Cambridge colleges in England—a very elderly nun in a habit told me to wait. The 'superior', that is the nun in charge of the convent, would be down to see me soon. Again, this was pretty much what I had expected.

But instead of being another French-speaking nun dressed in a habit, when the superior arrived, wearing ordinary European clothes, she spoke to me in fluent, colloquial English. (See Figure 1.9.) She offered me tea, and we sat in the convent's dining room—elegantly furnished in a surprisingly modern way—and I told her about my research project. She was plainly very interested in the archaeology of the Nazareth area and asked many well-informed questions. After we had spoken for a while about my work, she led me across the convent to see the 'Cellar'.

Entering one of the ranges of buildings around the front courtyard, we passed along a short corridor to a small antechamber which had a door on one side with a sign saying 'museum' and, through another door opposite it, we went down a broad flight of steps.

It was already obvious that this was going to be something different to what I had expected. The walls at the top of the steps were lined with shelves, on which were pieces of Byzantine and Crusader-period architectural stonework—column capitals (the frequently decorated tops of stone columns) and fragments of elaborately carved stone.

At the bottom of the steps lay a room brightly lit by electric lights, the walls of which were, to judge from the style of the stonework, built by the

Figure 1.9. The two convent superiors during the twenty-first-century fieldwork: Sister Margherita (left) and Sister Stefania, on the cloister terrace of the convent Photo: Ken Dark, with permission of the Sisters of Nazareth convent.

Figure 1.10. The Large Cave, the first of many surprises at the site on my initial visit. Photo: Ken Dark.

Crusaders. Above us was a fine example of the sort of cross-vault seen in medieval castles and churches in Europe. An arched medieval doorway led to a passageway off to the left.

But my guide wanted to show me what was on the right first. The whole wall on the right of the room consisted of a stone-built arch with a water cistern behind it cut deep into the rock. This, she said, was the well.

Then she led me forward through a high, rock-cut archway into a surprisingly big cave, which I later called the 'Large Cave' during my own work at the site. (See Figure 1.10.) The Large Cave was cut into the rock rather than being natural and was lit by a circular hole in the ceiling above its curved end. It looked like a cave-church, a type of structure widely found in the Byzantine world, including the Holy Land.

We walked along the cave, my guide pointing out details. (See Figure 1.11.) There were rock-cut graves, now empty, and steps up to the curved end of the cave.

When I came to examine the cave in detail the following year, and looked at the records of previous excavations within it, the graves turned out to be

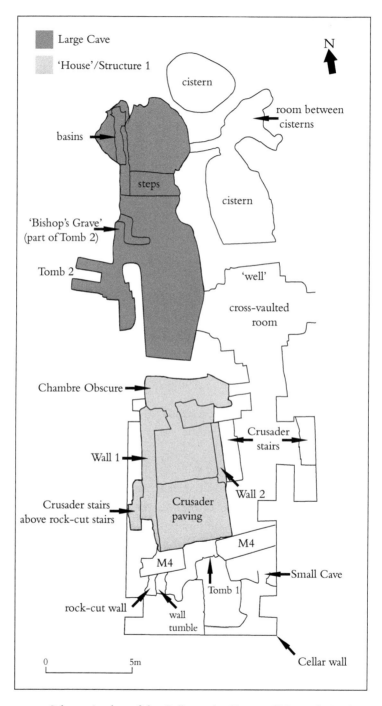

Figure 1.11. Schematic plan of the Cellar at the Sisters of Nazareth site (copyright Ken Dark), showing features often mentioned in this book. Note: this is just a diagram to explain where these features are located: for an accurate detailed plan of the Cellar, see Figure 0.4.

remnants of a rock-cut tomb, which during my work at the site I later called Tomb 2. We will come to Tomb 1 later in this chapter.

Why had I never read about this? Nothing I had seen even hinted at a cave-church surviving right in the middle of Nazareth.

But I knew that a Late Roman pilgrim, a Western woman called Egeria, had written about a cave-church in the 380s. She said it had a well, and was where the Virgin Mary had once lived.

A long rock-cut bench ran along the left side of the cave's curved end. This bench had a series of roughly rectangular basins cut into its surface, with small holes in their sides, which looked as if they were so that liquid could drain from one to another.

I could see that the cave-church was old—but how old? Was it Late Roman, Byzantine, or Crusader?

My train of thought was broken by my guide saying that she would then take me to see what I had really come for: the tomb. We went back along the cave, out into the antechamber with the well, and this time through the arch and along the vaulted passageway beyond it.

Walking through a corridor, its vaults and arched doorways again typical of the Crusaders, we turned right, through a doorway into a narrow dark room. This was, she said, the 'Chambre Obscure', French for 'dark room'.

I could see at once that the room had several different phases of construction. There were Crusader vaults and Crusader stonework lining the walls. But part of the walls was plainly earlier and cut out of the natural rock. At the end, there was a shallow, round-headed niche. It looked like a Byzantine prayer niche, used by monks as a focus for private prayer.

Hardly having time to take all this in, we turned left again through another doorway. This time the doorway was cut out of the rock. It led into a large space, where, just as you entered, there was what looked like a ruinous building, with rock-cut walls topped by stone-built walls, which seemed to be of a different date.

Unlike the Large Cave, there was no reason to suppose that this building had originally been underground. It looked as if it had been cut back into the hillside and had stood above ground when it was constructed. As on most archaeological sites, subsequent construction at the site and the gradual build-up of soil over the centuries would easily explain how it was buried. Especially in a city centre, like this, what was once the ground surface can be many metres deep today.

Standing in front of the longest rock-cut wall of the building—which I was to call 'Wall 1' when working on the site the following year—my guide told me that this was indeed considered by the nuns to have been a house. But some said it was more than an ordinary village residence.

She explained that a nineteenth-century biblical scholar had suggested that the lost Byzantine 'Church of the Nutrition'—'nutrition' in the sense of upbringing or nurturing—had been on the site of the convent. The Church of the Nutrition was described in a famous seventh-century pilgrimage account of Nazareth called *De Locis Sanctis* ('Concerning the Holy Places'), which said that the church was built over the house where Jesus had been brought up. She said that what we were looking at was claimed by some to be the very house.

Although I knew that such attributions to biblical figures were often only attested in the fourth century AD, and were of doubtful reliability, one thing about the 'house' struck me immediately. I had seen things like its rock-cut walls before, and they *were* places where people may have lived. Some of the quarries in the valley north of Nazareth had been reused in the Roman period as buildings, with drystone walls and broken pieces of Roman pottery strewn around them.

The rock-cut walls in the Cellar may have been something of that sort, I thought. What was more, the longest rock-cut wall and the earliest, rock-cut part of the Chambre Obscure could be seen as forming a two-roomed structure, which I later called 'Structure 1'. (See Figure 1.12.)

To make Structure 1 into a building, it would have needed other walls filling the gaps between those cut out of the rock. Behind me, as I looked at Wall 1, there was what might be evidence for this. Another wall, this time built of stone, faced Wall 1.

This facing wall, which I called 'Wall 2' during my later work on the site, had characteristics of its construction suggesting a Crusader date. There was what looked like medieval paving on part of the floor of the 'house', and there were Crusader-period stairways in the same part of the Cellar. When working on the site in subsequent years, it was possible to show that the paving was also Crusader in date.

But Wall 2 could, I realized, have replaced or incorporated an earlier stone-built wall and so have been another part of Structure 1. It turned out, as we shall see in Chapter 5, that this might well have been the case.

So even then it seemed possible that Structure 1 might really be a house, in the sense of a place where someone lived. If it was, then it might be a

Figure 1.12. The 'house' Structure 1, at the Sisters of Nazareth site. Looking north towards the doorway into the Chambre Obscure. Photo: Ken Dark.

Roman house right in the middle of Nazareth—a place where no surface-built Roman-period houses had then ever been found. I leant against Wall 2, looking through what was left of a stone window frame.

I wondered what all this could mean. Why had I never heard of the site? Obviously, before embarking on my research project I had read everything I could find about the archaeology of Nazareth and the Roman-period and Byzantine Galilee where it is located. That is just a matter of archaeological due diligence.

But some things get published in obscure places—it is always possible that, no matter how hard you try, and which libraries you can access, you'll miss one or two sites. I thought that must be what had happened here. After all, being a secular archaeologist rather than a biblical scholar, I could have missed it in one of the many journals intended for scholars of religion. Probably, I thought, it was published in such a place—maybe in the nineteenth century, when European archaeologists were digging all over the Holy Land.

Moving on, we went through a gap in a massive well-built wall, much thicker than an ordinary house wall. This—which the nuns called M4 ('M' for 'mur', the French word for wall)—ran straight across the south end of the Cellar. From its construction, it also appeared to be medieval in date. Beyond it was a modern timber walkway leading down to the tomb which I had originally come to the site to see, and which was later called by me 'Tomb 1'.

This tomb was a very well-preserved example of the usual type of rock-cut Jewish tombs made in the Early Roman period. The superior said that some people thought it was first century BC; some that it was first century AD. All had agreed it was earlier than the 'house', that is earlier than Structure 1.

As an archaeologist, it was obvious to me that it was impossible for Structure 1 to be later than the tomb. The construction of the tomb had plainly cut through Structure 1, so the tomb was obviously the later of the two. But, at least at first sight, a first-century AD date for the tomb looked about right.

If so, then Structure 1 was earlier than a first-century tomb. If it was Roman period at all, it really could belong to the first century AD. Was this actually a house from Jesus' Nazareth?

At the top of the steps, the superior unlocked the museum door and we entered. The room had obviously been fitted out as a proper museum some

Figure 1.13. The convent museum, as it was in 2005, and during the 2006–10 survey of the Cellar. Photo: Ken Dark.

time previously. (See Figure 1.13.) Although it had clearly seen better days, it was packed with archaeological material. There were coins, pottery lamps and bowls, and glass vessels in display cabinets, and large pieces of white marble and sculpted limestone on the floor. Among the column capitals and column shafts, a Byzantine marble screen from a church immediately caught my attention.

Looking around the museum, although some of the labels no longer matched the exhibits, I was stunned. If even only a fraction of this came from the site, then this was going to be a remarkably useful resource for my research project.

In one corner of the room there was a simple wooden desk and chair. My guide stood behind it as I finished looking around. 'I had no idea this was all here; do you know where it's published?' I asked.

She took a brief photocopied leaflet from the desk. 'This is the most recent publication,' she told me. It was a very short article from the 1980 issue of a magazine of biblical studies, written by a European priest and accompanied by a very sketchy plan. When I expressed astonishment, she assured me that, while people had dug there for over a century, none of them had ever published their excavations in an academic journal, let alone a book.

This would make the perfect site in Nazareth to answer the key remaining questions of my research project. There was no need even to dig.

I asked if it might be possible to include this site in my project, expecting an immediate rejection. But to my surprise she said that it might be possible, but would need the approval of the Order, the governing body for all of the Sisters of Nazareth convents, based in Paris. She told me to send her a letter setting out exactly what I had in mind, what the convent could expect from me, and what I would expect from them. This would be needed to get the approval of the Order in Paris. After a brief further discussion of some practicalities, I left the convent.

Later that year, after an exchange of emails about my project and plans for work at the site, the convent and Sisters of Nazareth Order in Paris gave permission for my work there. Following further permission from the Israel Antiquities Authority, which regulates archaeological research in Israel, my team started work at the convent in December 2006.

So that was how, quite by chance, I became a sort of accidental biblical archaeologist, working on first-century Nazareth as well as its later Roman and Byzantine successors.

However, before we can get to what was found at the Sisters of Nazareth, it is important to put the site in the wider context of the landscape and archaeology of Nazareth. This, which is necessary to understand more fully the Sisters of Nazareth evidence, is the subject of the next chapter.

2

Pilgrims, monks, and digs

Nazareth is undoubtedly one of the most famous places in the twenty-first-century world. It is known to Christians and non-Christians alike, if only through the phrase 'Jesus of Nazareth' as an alternative name for Jesus Christ. Yet its archaeology has been very little studied. Indeed, there can be few, if any, such famous locations that have been so neglected by archaeologists for such a long time.

This chapter considers what is known about Nazareth in the first century AD from written sources and from archaeology, apart from the Sisters of Nazareth site which is the subject of the next three chapters. Another good starting point for discussing an archaeological site is its natural environment in the past and present. This will also be considered in the present chapter.

Written sources for ancient Nazareth

Nazareth is so famous today that it might seem obvious that it was written about extensively in the past. But this is a mistaken premise. Why should anyone during the Roman period, other than Christians, consider it worth writing about an obscure Galilean village?

No one bothered to write about the vast majority of the many thousands of villages in the Roman Empire. Modern scholars don't even know the names of most of these settlements, nor of any of their inhabitants.

The first mention of Nazareth as a place is by the writers of the Christian Gospels. It would be—because they were the first people that we know of who had any reason to be interested in it!

We can put the Gospels' references to Nazareth in context by considering mentions of Nazareth over the following thousand years. These form a very informative pattern.

After the canonical Gospels (those conventionally used in the Christian Bible), Nazareth is mentioned next in the second-century apocryphal Gospel of Thomas and the third-century Protoevangelium of James. In addition, Eusebius, a Christian writer and historian living in the fourth century, says that he got part of his information about Nazareth from another second-century writer called Hegesippus.

According to Eusebius—who, historians usually agree, wasn't making up his source for this comment—Hegesippus referred to relatives of Jesus living in the Galilean villages of Nazareth and Kokhba in later centuries.

Whether, of course, Hegesippus was mistaken, we can't be sure, but the late second- and third-century writer Julius Africanus also mentions relatives of Jesus—in the same sense—living in Nazareth and Kokhaba. The latter is almost certainly Hegesippus' Kokhba, and both are identifiable with the village of Kaukab, north of Nazareth.

Early Roman-period evidence from Kaukab indicates a settlement there. Regardless of whether relatives of Jesus, or people who said that they were relatives of Jesus, lived there in the Roman period, it is at least likely to have been a real village at that time.

It is hard to know what to make of these references to Jesus' second-century relatives. What we do know is that they certainly weren't believed to be actually descendants of Jesus, but of Mary's other sons. If Mary had other children, it might be expected that their descendants would be living in Galilee in the second century, so this in itself isn't that surprising.

The same sort of story is also mentioned in a slightly later text called the *Martyrdom of Conon*. The *Martyrdom* says that during the Roman emperor Decius' persecution of the Christians in 250–1, an old gardener working on an imperial estate was martyred close to Magydos in Pamphylia. It is said that this gardener, called Conon, claimed that he was from 'Nazareth in Galilee . . . of the family of Christ, whose worship I have inherited from my ancestors'.

The whole story could be fictitious, of course, but there was an imperial estate at Magydos in Pamphylia—so maybe the writer of the *Martyrdom* really did know something factual. We shall encounter the name Conon again later in this chapter.

Consequently, we have several Christian mentions of Nazareth after the Gospels but during the Roman period. Their significance for the history of early Christianity may be debatable, but they consistently mention Nazareth as a settlement—that is, somewhere people lived.

Both the Jewish *Midrash Kohelet*—a religious text—and an inscription (the 'Caesarea Inscription'), found at an important Roman town on what is today the northern coast of Israel, refer to a Jewish priestly family residing in Roman-period Nazareth. Priestly families fled to Galilee as refugees from Jerusalem in the late first century, so this is again something which is quite credible. But we hear no more about this from any other written source.

One of the best-known 'biblical archaeologists' in late twentieth- and early twenty-first-century America, James Strange, thought that the Jewish writer Eleazar Ha-Kalir's *Lamentations* also referred to first- or second-century Nazareth. That said, the surviving version only dates to somewhere between the sixth and ninth centuries, so it is of doubtful significance.

All this suggests that only those with a particular interest in Nazareth—either as the home of Jesus or, later, the residence of a priestly family from Jerusalem—considered it worth mentioning. This isn't in the least surprising, because it is typical of most other Roman-period villages in Galilee, or for that matter in the Roman provinces generally.

As already mentioned, although Nazareth is famous today, there is no reason to suppose that it was famous to anyone but Christians until Christianity was supported, rather than oppressed, by the Roman authorities. That wasn't until the early fourth century.

What is actually surprising is that in the fourth century even Roman Christians, who might be expected to refer to Nazareth, hardly mention it at all. If they do, they often refer to the place dismissively. For example, the celebrated fourth-century Christian bishop, and prolific author, John Chrysostom only mentions the Nazareth of his own time once. Then he dismisses it as 'a miserable village'. Another eminent Christian writer—no less than the translator of the Bible into Latin—Jerome, tells us that Nazareth was only 'a small village'.

If both these men, considered saints by the Eastern Orthodox and Catholic Churches, could disregard Nazareth as a settlement, then we should perhaps be unsurprised by the stunning lack of interest shown in it by anyone else writing texts which survive today.

Even Christian pilgrims coming to Galilee in the Late Roman and Byzantine periods, and referring to every little stop on their way, usually fail to mention Nazareth. For example, 'the Bordeaux Pilgrim', who wrote the earliest surviving pilgrim account of the Holy Land, omits to mention Nazareth at all.

Anyone could get the impression from these writings that Nazareth was of little or no importance to Roman-period or Byzantine Christians. These pilgrims considered many, many specific locations holy and tell us about them. But they mostly ignore Nazareth.

However, there is no doubt that Nazareth was there throughout all of this. Two fourth-century accounts describe it.

The first is the *Panarion*, written by bishop Epiphanius in the 370s. This says that when Joseph of Tiberias (Tiberius is a town on the western shore of the Sea of Galilee), a Jewish official in the Roman imperial administration, became a Christian, he commanded churches to be established in both Nazareth and Sepphoris. Epiphanius tells us that both places were wholly Jewish communities—although we know from archaeology that this was far from the case at Sepphoris, where there was a pagan temple.

Although Epiphanius was certainly mistaken about Sepphoris' exclusively Jewish character in the Late Roman period, it is possible that Joseph of Tiberius did build churches in Nazareth and the town. Late Roman officials did so elsewhere, and if Joseph was associated with Galilee, this might seem a logical location for him to make an architectural statement of his faith.

The other description is much more helpful for understanding Late Roman Nazareth. This was written by a woman called Egeria, a pilgrim from the Western Roman Empire—possibly Spain—who went to the Holy Land in about 383. Egeria is the first person to provide us with a more detailed description of Nazareth.

As has already been mentioned in Chapter 1, Egeria says that there was a big cave in Nazareth, used as a church because it was where the Virgin Mary had lived in the first century. Egeria gives one more detail of this cave. She says that 'within the actual cave is the place from which she drew water'. This might seem a trivial observation, but it is important in locating the cave because Nazareth is very poorly provided with natural water sources.

According to Egeria, there was also what she describes as a synagogue turned into a church and 'a garden in which the Lord used to be after his return from Egypt'. These are, to put it mildly, enigmatic features. We hear no more of a synagogue turned into a church in Nazareth until the Crusader period. Egeria is the only writer to mention the garden. She also says that there was a well outside the village associated with the Virgin Mary.

What is certain from all this is that by the 380s Nazareth had become a place of Christian pilgrimage. It had various attractions for pilgrims to see, such as the garden, wells, and two churches. This also confirms that, at least by that time, places within the village were being identified as associated with Jesus' childhood.

But Egeria's is the last mention of Nazareth for over seventy years. Even then, when Nazareth is listed as the seat of a bishop in 460, we are told only that the bishop was under the authority of a senior bishop based at Scythopolis. Scythopolis was an important Roman town, flourishing as a Christian community in the fifth and sixth centuries. Its impressive ruins, today known as Beth Shean, about 30 kilometres south-east of Nazareth, are a popular destination for twenty-first-century tourists.

To have had a bishop in 460 implies that Nazareth had at least one impressive church—all Byzantine bishops had these, their cathedrals—and probably that this church was surrounded by a complex of residential and administrative buildings for the bishop and his staff. Again, these are usual in the Byzantine Empire.

However, neither the bishop of Nazareth, nor his church, are *ever* again mentioned in Byzantine written sources. If an important Church official and a massive church can be absent from texts written in the deeply Christian Byzantine world over the subsequent century and a half of Byzantine rule in Nazareth, this should highlight how extremely limited written sources are in telling us anything about this settlement.

That point is reinforced by the total absence of any written evidence for Nazareth over the following 110 years. It is only in about 570 that we even have another pilgrim account. That is, there is a century of complete silence about Nazareth from surviving texts, although we know it was an important place for the Byzantine Church, and cathedrals weren't typically built in small villages.

Another anonymous pilgrim, known to historians as 'the Piacenza Pilgrim', describes Nazareth in around 570 as a Christian pilgrimage site with a 'synagogue'—it is unclear if this is the one which Egeria mentioned—and a 'house of Saint Mary...now a basilica'. The term 'basilica' was often used by the sixth century for a church with a rectangular nave and an apse at one end.

The latter cannot be Egeria's cave-church, as it would be almost impossible to turn a cave-church into an above-ground congregational hall which a sixth-century pilgrim would call a basilica. Nor is it probably Egeria's synagogue turned into a church, because it was meant to be a house turned into a church rather than a synagogue turned into a church.

Likewise, although the Piacenza Pilgrim mentions that there was a Jewish community in sixth-century Nazareth, it is unlikely that a Jewish synagogue would be singled out for mention, when the pilgrim would have come across Jewish synagogues throughout their stay in the Holy Land.

So, either the Piacenza Pilgrim is describing a different set of buildings to those of the 380s—which might be unsurprising after about 200 years—or the synagogue was the one already turned into a church by Egeria's time. After the Piacenza Pilgrim, we once again hear no more about Nazareth for decades.

In fact, the next mention of Byzantine Nazareth concerns the Persian invasion of the Holy Land in the early seventh century. This doesn't contain anything about the settlement as a place, but only comments on how its Jewish inhabitants sided with the Persians. Even that observation is open to debate.

Then there is another hiatus in our written sources for Nazareth for over half a century. In fact, this one extends beyond the end of the period of Byzantine rule in Galilee. In the late seventh century, perhaps about 670, Adomnán, the abbot of the important monastery at Iona, an island off the west coast of Scotland, wrote a pilgrimage account called *De Locis Sanctis* ('Concerning the Holy Places').

The sources for Adomnán's account are a matter of scholarly controversy. Although he presents it as, in effect, something dictated to him by a Frankish pilgrim called Arculf, this was probably just a literary device—his style of writing. It is most likely that Adomnán wrote the whole thing himself.

This presents a different problem for the historian. It is certain that Adomnán used existing descriptions of the Holy Land as a model for some parts of his text. But by no means all. For others he had what seem to be up-to-date eyewitness descriptions. Either he had been there himself recently, which is quite plausible, or he was informed by someone who had.

One of the passages in the text falling into the eyewitness category is a description of Nazareth. Adomnán says that it contained two large churches, one built over the site of the Annunciation and another built on the site of the house where Jesus was brought up by Joseph and Mary. He gives a description of the latter church, which he says was in the centre of seventh-century Nazareth.

Although Nazareth was under Muslim rule, rather than that of the Christian Byzantine Empire, in the 720s we have two more written descriptions of Nazareth. In that decade, the Muslim ruler Yazid II ordered the destruction of images in Nazareth's churches. A pilgrim account also shows that there was at least one active church, although Christians had to keep up payments to avoid it being destroyed.

Despite this worsening political situation, Nazareth evidently continued to draw Christian attention into the ninth century. The Arab geographer Al-Mas´ūdī describes Christian religious practices at a tomb in a Nazareth church. Christians were apparently venerating the tomb because they believed it to be the grave of a saint.

Al-Mas´ūdī was also the first to suggest that Jesus' Nazareth was anywhere other than in Galilee. Rather than the village identified with it since the Roman period, Al-Mas´ūdī claims that people—presumably people other than Christians—said that it was at Nasarah near al-Lajun. However, the Gospels make it clear that their Nazareth is a place in Galilee, and al-Lajun is south-east of the Dead Sea, and so far away from Galilee.

The next reference to Nazareth in a written source is as late as 1010. Then, the Church of the Annunciation was destroyed on the caliph's orders. What 'destroyed' means in this context may be debated, but nothing more is said of Nazareth until 1099, when it was captured by Crusader forces and its churches subsequently restored. The Crusader capture of Nazareth forms a convenient place to end this review of textual references.

What is striking from reviewing all the mentions of Nazareth in written sources is just how few they are. There are gaps of decades—three of 70, 110, and 89 years—when there are no references to Nazareth at all.

These gaps occur when Nazareth was already a Christian pilgrimage centre. They concern somewhere that was by that time—the 390s to 1090s—one of the most well-known places in the world to many people living in Europe and the Middle East. This has an important implication for the lack of references to Nazareth in earlier written sources.

First-century Nazareth is better attested in written sources than the Christian pilgrimage centre of Nazareth was in later centuries. That is, it would be ridiculous to claim that the absence of more written attestations to Nazareth in the first century means that no settlement of that name existed then.

What is more, there is a remarkable consistency regarding where all of these writers—apart from Al-Mas´ūdī—say that Nazareth was located. To the Gospel writers, the early Christians of the second to fourth centuries, the pilgrims of the Late Roman period, and those who described the relocation of the Jewish priestly families, Nazareth was in Galilee.

Nor do any of these written sources give us any reason to doubt that first-century Nazareth was somewhere under the modern city of the same name. The earliest specific identifications of Nazareth within Galilee—deriving from the Roman period—support this. As we shall see, so does the history of the churches in what is currently central Nazareth. No other candidates have ever been credibly presented.

Consequently, although written evidence from later centuries cannot reliably add to the Gospels' brief description of first-century Nazareth, it offers no evidence to doubt that there *was* a historical settlement of Nazareth, and that it was on the site of the present city. Indeed, that there were long gaps between written accounts of Nazareth may be the most informative evidence, so far as the history of Nazareth is concerned, deriving from these post-biblical texts. These gaps show that we cannot take a lack of written references to Nazareth as significant for estimating its size or the character of its occupation.

It is, therefore, up to the study of material evidence, that is to archaeological research, to provide further evidence for first-century Nazareth. Most of this evidence derives from buildings, graves, and portable objects such as pottery, but although this was briefly mentioned in Chapter 1, it is worth returning to the subject of Nazareth's natural environment and its implications for first-century settlement and economy.

Natural Nazareth

One of the most noticeable characteristics of Nazareth is that it lies on limestone, 'chalk', hills. Most of these hills are covered by rich brown soils, although where the rock is exposed other, more or less white, soils can be seen. A red soil can be seen on some of the hills.

Rainfall was sufficient for very productive agriculture. At about 50–80 millimetres annually, the amount of rainfall in Nazareth is similar to some parts of Britain.

These are perfect circumstances to produce the crops that were staples of most people's diet in the lands bordering the Mediterranean Sea until recently: wheat, barley, grapes, and olives. Grass on the hills could also feed sheep, cattle, and goats, providing the farmers with meat, milk, cheese, and yoghurt.

Judging from what was grown there in later centuries, a wide variety of fruit and vegetables could also be produced. Written sources for Galilee suggest, among other fruit and vegetables, apples, pears, pomegranates, figs, onions, and legumes—peas and beans.

This could, of course, be the basis for a very healthy diet. So long as farmers were allowed to keep at least some of their produce, this, in turn, suggests that there is no reason to suppose dietary deficiencies or malnutrition were commonplace.

The agricultural wealth of Galilee in general was certainly something visitors commented on again and again throughout the last two thousand years. For example, the sixth-century 'Piacenza Pilgrim' considered the Nazareth area 'a paradise... in its wheat and fruit... surpassing even Egypt in its wine, oil and apples'. Medieval and modern travellers made similar comments.

The hills were also well wooded. Today, the woodland has been largely removed—although patches to the west and north of Nazareth remain—but as late as the nineteenth century there was a lot more.

The trees were probably oak (Tabor oak and Kermes oak) and Aleppo pine—which were good for building—and terebinth. So, timber components to buildings, or even wholly timber structures, might be expected. Certainly, there was no lack of long and sturdy timber to provide good roofs and indoor posts to support considerable roof spans.

Nevertheless, while often covered with grass or other vegetation, some parts of the hills remain bare white rock. In this exposed rock, hillsides are dotted with natural caves. These are mostly small and have only a single chamber. Some are open to the air; others are inaccessible, so that they form underground voids invisible from the present land surface.

Small springs and seasonal rivers (wadis) supply water to people and farm animals in this landscape. In summer the wadis are completely dry, forming valleys which could be used as seasonal trackways, their beds relatively free of obstacles. If somebody knew the route of a wadi, they could have used it as a natural pathway.

Until the nineteenth century, a wadi of this sort ran through what is today the centre of modern Nazareth. Its line was up the present street immediately outside the Church of the Annunciation, passing under what is today the Franciscan Catholic pilgrim hostel called Casa Nova, which means 'new house', built in 1837. Physical evidence of this wadi was discovered when the hostel was rebuilt in 1863, and also when the Church of the Annunciation was being rebuilt in the 1960s.

The Nazareth wadi must have been one of the most distinctive landscape features in the whole area before it was infilled. Around the wadi there were lesser hills and crags. There were higher hills to the north and west, but to the east the land was flatter. On this flatter ground there was a more substantial spring, today called Mary's (or St Mary's) Well. (See Figure 2.1.) This is about 17 metres to the north of the present Greek Orthodox church of St Gabriel, where it emerges in an elliptical rock-cut cave. As early as the 380s, Egeria mentions that the well was used by the Virgin Mary, and this continues to be widely believed, hence its name.

In later centuries the water from this well was channelled to an elaborate well house to the south. This well house has been rebuilt in a non-functional way as a modern tourist attraction.

In the nineteenth century Mary's Well was the main well of Nazareth. It has often been assumed that this was so in the first century. But other smaller

Figure 2.1. The modern reconstruction of Mary's Well. From *Roman-period and Byzantine Nazareth and its hinterland*, 1st ed., by Ken Dark, copyright 2020 by Imprint; reproduced by permission of Taylor & Francis Group.

springs existed to the west and north, and these could have provided water for a first-century village rather than a nineteenth-century town.

In Roman-period Galilee many settlements used water supplies outside their limits, some as much as 1.5 kilometres away. Others depended on their inhabitants collecting rain during the winter and storing this in rock-cut cisterns.

Many Galilean settlements used this system in the Roman period, such as Yodefat, Shikhin, and Khirbet Qana. This type of water collection is even attested from nineteenth-century observations. For example, two villages—Mashad and Daburiyyah—near Nazareth were supplied with drinking water in just such a way.

Another misconception has been that the hills encompassed within modern Nazareth would have prevented settlement in the area. This is disproved by archaeological evidence from other sites in Galilee. Other first-century villages were built on hillslopes, as at Khirbet Qana. There, terraced ranks of houses ran up the hillside, with others on the top.

Terraces were also built for agriculture on hillslopes around Nazareth, and used from ancient times until today. At the Nazareth Village, or Nazareth Village Farm (NVF), excavation, in the grounds of a modern hospital just outside what is today central Nazareth, there were two types of terraces in use in the first century.

Dry terraces provided farmers with approximately flat areas of well-drained aerated soil, probably for vegetables and perhaps fruit trees. Wet terraces were irrigated by conduits and cisterns for crops needing more water. As the archaeologists at the Nazareth Village excavation said, these might have supported olives, grapes, figs, almonds, wheat, and barley.

This recalls the range of crops grown in the Nazareth area in the nineteenth century. Roman olive presses at the Nazareth Village site, and in the countryside around Nazareth, also provide evidence of olive-growing. Likewise, Roman wine presses found in the centre of modern Nazareth at the Church of the Annunciation site and in the valley to its north attest the cultivation of grapes.

There is evidence from the excavation at the International Marian Center (IMC) site in central Nazareth, discussed later in this chapter, that people in first-century Nazareth kept cattle, sheep, and/or goats. Consequently, there is good reason to interpret the first-century landscape around Nazareth as dominated by mixed farming—the keeping of farm animals and the cultivation of wheat, barley, fruit, and vegetables, along with olive groves and vineyards. The manufacture of wine and olive oil is attested by the wine and olive presses.

To build up a better picture of what that landscape looked like, it is also, of course, necessary to factor in human settlements. Fortunately, a combination of Israeli rescue archaeology and archaeological survey by my own team enables us to do just that.

Roman-period rural settlement around Nazareth

Israeli archaeologists have excavated several Roman-period settlements in Nahal Zippori (the broad valley between Sepphoris to the north and Nazareth) in the course of 'rescue' projects ahead of construction work. Because of the reason for their excavations, much of this has been directed towards rapidly expanding modern communities in the valley: Reina, Moshav Zippori, 'Illut and 'Ein Zippori.

It turns out that all of these modern communities are on the sites of Roman-period settlements. In Moshav Zippori, a village close to Sepphoris national park, rescue work by the Israel Antiquities Authority (IAA) and studies by other Israeli archaeologists have discovered Roman-period buildings, cisterns, and tombs along with what is probably evidence of glass-working and, perhaps, other manufacturing activities. Two artificial pools might also have been associated with manufacturing, or could have been for agriculture. Recently, a pottery kiln, dated to the Roman period, was excavated there.

Quarrying also took place in what is today Moshav Zippori in the Early Roman period. But, although it might seem surprising, the Moshav Zippori quarries appear to have been inhabited. The evidence for this comes from two IAA rescue excavations.

The first excavation found quarries dating from the Roman period. One of two caves created by this quarrying had plastered walls and sockets for a door. A cistern, also with plastered walls, was associated with this. The cistern could have been to provide water for workers, but if the cave was just a storeroom for tools—a quarry workers' 'lock-up'—then there is no reason why it would be plastered. So, it seems to have been a place where people lived, if only temporarily while working in the adjacent quarry.

The second excavation also found evidence of a structure associated with quarrying. This time, a wall 5 metres long was cut out of the rock and its surface smoothed. Mortared stone walls were built to form the other sides of a rectangular room, 2.8 metres high, with a slightly sunken floor. A rock-cut column was retained in the south-east corner of the room, probably to hold up the roof. This was obviously more than a storeroom or stable.

Activity inside this structure was associated with Roman-period cooking pots and their Byzantine equivalents, suggesting a lengthy duration of human use, probably involving the consumption of food. Again, this appears to be a place where people actually lived, over a matter of centuries.

Both structures may be interpreted as domestic huts, almost certainly occupied by quarry workers. This would explain the plastered walls, pottery, hinged door, and the effort expended on constructing them. Their association with the workers quarrying the stone is implied by the fact that elements of their design—such as the column of rock probably used as a roof support—would only have been possible if the decision to construct them was made prior to quarrying.

In a Roman-period Jewish context, domestic habitation and burial were usually kept apart. It is, then, surprising to find that this small-scale occupation was close to one of Sepphoris' main cemeteries. Sited nearby but separate from the structures, this included both rock-cut tombs and some prestigious graves—notably that of Rabbi Yehuda Ben Halevi, whose burial is recorded on an inscription.

The presence of the cemetery may also indicate a close relationship between the Roman-period settlement at Moshav Zippori and Sepphoris. Sepphoris is known from written sources to have had a least one dependent village just outside it.

In Reina, a village so close to modern Nazareth that it is almost a suburb of the city, IAA rescue excavation has also found that this modern village is the site of a substantial Roman-period settlement. This settlement is distinguished from many similarly sized villages in Roman Galilee by showing evidence of the production of limestone objects, including various sorts of vessels. Limestone vessels were made in Roman-period Jewish contexts in Galilee because limestone was believed to be unaffected by ritual impurity.

Consequently, limestone vessels could be used for anything which was to be kept, in that sense, pure, and then reused over and over again. Stone vessels of this type have been found in Sepphoris, Nazareth, and at several sites in the valley between them.

Also very near modern Nazareth, another Roman-period village has been found by the IAA at 'Illut. This is a place that has been identified on the basis of written sources as perhaps Ayyatalu, where one of the priestly families came as refugees from the destruction of the Second Temple at Jerusalem.

The evidence from this area resembles that from Moshav Zippori, in that it includes domestic structures, rock-cut tombs, and artificial pools, although the pools were interpreted by the excavator at this site as evidence of fish-breeding rather than agriculture. Whether this was so, other IAA rescue excavations have found well-preserved Hellenistic and Roman-period house walls, standing over 1.5 metres high.

The other most substantial Roman-period settlement in the valley is at 'Ein Zippori, which is at the most productive of the many springs between Nazareth and Sepphoris, an obvious place for settlement in all periods. Roman-period evidence from near the well dates from the first century BC onward, and includes walls, a water cistern, a water conduit, and quarrying. A small structure might be interpreted as an agricultural watchtower, of the sort also evidenced from excavations within Nazareth.

All of these settlements present a fairly consistent picture of Roman-period settlement in the valley between Nazareth and Sepphoris. They all show evidence of agriculture and quarrying, supplemented by manufacturing activities. The latter included glass-making and the production of limestone objects, especially vessels to hold liquids.

This evidence is supplemented by two studies of all previously recorded sites in the valley, undertaken before my own work there—described briefly in Chapter 1—started in 2004. At that time, far fewer Roman-period settlements were known in the valley than we subsequently found, but it was already apparent that this part of Nahal Zippori was farmed and settled with agricultural villages and smaller settlements, probably farms, from the start of the Roman period onward.

Combining these earlier studies and excavations with my own survey, it is apparent that the valley between Sepphoris and Nazareth (hereafter just called 'the valley' in this book) was very densely settled compared to many other areas of Galilee. Most of these settlements were small, probably representing family farms, but as we have seen at 'Illut, Moshav Zippori, Reina, and 'Ein Zippori, larger communities, probably small villages, were also present.

At this point we may conveniently turn to what is known of the archaeology of Roman-period Nazareth itself, apart from the Sisters of Nazareth site—which will be discussed in more detail in subsequent chapters.

Archaeological knowledge of Roman Nazareth

During the nineteenth century anyone might have thought, using just the archaeological evidence, that Roman Nazareth was a city of the dead. Almost all of the archaeological evidence dating to the Roman period then published from Nazareth consisted of Jewish rock-cut tombs and the objects found within them.

The rapid expansion of Nazareth between 1850 and 1950 led to many burial places being discovered by accident. Being rock-cut chambers containing skeletons and easily recognizable objects, such as complete glass vessels, these tombs were hard to miss even for untrained workmen.

Before World War I, a local historian summed up this evidence, saying that there were three types of Roman-period tombs in Nazareth: *kokhim* tombs, 'sarcophagi in caves', and 'tombs cut in the face of the rock'. *Kokhim* tombs are rock-cut underground chambers with a series of narrow slots (*loculi*) in the walls for the individual graves. Some had an entrance courtyard, also cut in the rock.

Most of the tombs found in central Nazareth at that time are only known from brief notes in nineteenth-century publications. Other than at the Sisters of Nazareth, the only one for which much more detail is available was found about 30 metres from the immediate predecessor of the current Church of the Annunciation.

This tomb comprised a rock-cut chamber with thirteen *loculi* and a stone disc (a 'rolling stone') blocking its entrance. The tomb was in use in the Roman period, judging from the objects found within it, but was probably constructed during the first century AD. On the basis of well-dated sites elsewhere, for example in the Jerusalem area and near Nazareth at Migdal ha'Emeq, the use of large stone discs—as at this tomb—apparently ceased after the end of that century.

Later Roman and Byzantine tombs sometimes had stone discs, but the discs were much smaller and there are other constructional details which differentiate them from the earlier ones. However, none of the later type is known to have been found in Nazareth itself.

Consequently, there is no reason to doubt that all of the Nazareth *kokhim* tombs were constructed in the Early Roman period, although often used until much later. The objects found in them suggest that they were high-status burials.

This would mean that Nazareth has far more of these burials than might be expected if it was simply a small agricultural hamlet. But whereas Roman-period high-status tombs are sometimes associated with inscriptions commemorating the dead, only three Roman inscriptions have even been claimed to come from Nazareth.

Probably the least interesting of these is a Greek-inscribed tombstone. This was probably brought to the Church of the Annunciation site to build a Crusader-period wall. The reuse of earlier stonework, including inscriptions and sarcophagi (stone coffins), is common in medieval buildings, including at Sepphoris.

The most celebrated of the Roman-period inscriptions said to have been found in Nazareth is, aptly enough, called the 'Nazareth Inscription'. It is an inscribed marble slab—claimed to be from Nazareth—with a long text apparently recording an imperial Roman decree forbidding tomb-robbing. Since its first publication in 1930, this has excited considerable interest among people hoping that it attests the Resurrection of Jesus.

However, a recent study using isotopic analysis of the marble has shown that it probably comes from the Greek island of Kos. Of course, the marble block could have been brought to Galilee and then inscribed, but it is at least suspicious that the tomb of the second-century BC ruler of Kos, Nikias, was infamously desecrated in the reign of the emperor Augustus. Such an event might have led to a proclamation in Kos by the Roman emperor against the removal of bodies from tombs. The inscription might have been brought to Nazareth only in the modern period.

The 'Nazareth Inscription' could also be an outright fake—although this may be less likely—or have come from the cemetery at Sepphoris rather than Nazareth. With its citizens usually loyal to the empire, Sepphoris might well have enacted the Roman law of *violatio sepulchri*—'tomb violation'—on which the inscription is based.

The 'Nazareth Inscription' is probably Early Roman in date. It may even date from the first century AD. However, its association with Nazareth, let alone the possibility that it refers to the Resurrection, is highly questionable.

The third inscription that has been attributed to Nazareth is a Roman military tombstone. It probably commemorated a member of the *Legio IV Flavia*, one of the legions of the Roman army. *Legio IV Flavia* was established by the Roman emperor Vespasian in AD 70, so roughly a generation after Jesus' crucifixion. The legion was based in Dalmatia, modern Croatia, but it could have been sent to suppress the Second Jewish Revolt.

The Second Jewish Revolt, between AD 132 and 135, was a major crisis for the Roman Empire, which sent many troops to combat it. Although this might account for the tombstone being in Galilee, its attribution to Nazareth is in doubt. It is very unlikely that a Roman military tombstone would have been set up at a Jewish village. Usually, Roman legionary tombstones are found in the cemeteries of major Roman towns or forts. More plausibly, then, if the tombstone is from the Nazareth area, it might have come from the extensive cemeteries of pro-Roman Sepphoris. Anyway, it is second-century if genuine and irrelevant to first-century Nazareth.

Consequently, there are no inscriptions from Nazareth that shed any light on the first-century settlement there. This is only what would be expected—first-century Jewish settlements in Galilee seldom have evidence of this sort.

The Church of the Annunciation

Archaeological excavation provides much better evidence for first-century Nazareth. The largest twentieth-century excavation in Nazareth was at the Church of the Annunciation, the cathedral-size church in central Nazareth. (See Figure 2.2.) The church is in a walled compound containing an extensive complex of other buildings, including paved courtyards and a covered walkway, another church—the Church of St Joseph—a school, a museum, and a Franciscan monastery. Much of this area has been excavated since the late nineteenth century.

Excavation began at the church in 1892, directed by Prosper Viaud and Benedict Vlaminck. But it was only when it was rebuilt in the second half of the twentieth century that the whole area beneath the present building was excavated. This rescue excavation was directed by Bellarmino Bagatti and took place principally between 1955 and 1966.

Bagatti must have seemed a perfect man for the job. He was a Catholic priest, a Franciscan monk, and a prominent member of the Franciscan school of biblical archaeology, based at Jerusalem. He had previously directed several important excavations in Rome and elsewhere in the Holy Land, and written academic work on Nazareth since the 1930s. His knowledge of the archaeology and religious history of Galilee was combined with a specific research interest in Nazareth.

However, Bagatti's interest in Nazareth was derived from his role in formulating, along with Emanuele Testa, the so-called 'Jewish-Christian'

Figure 2.2. The present Church of the Annunciation in Nazareth. From *Roman-period and Byzantine Nazareth and its hinterland*, 1st ed., by Ken Dark, copyright 2020 by Imprint; reproduced by permission of Taylor & Francis Group.

hypothesis of Christian origins. In briefest form, this held that a distinctive set of beliefs and religious practices characterized the earliest post-biblical followers of Jesus. One of the most important Jewish-Christian communities, Bagatti and Testa argued, was in Nazareth.

Consequently, Bagatti investigated the archaeology of Nazareth with this specific interpretation of its archaeology in mind. He was also less than up to date in his excavation techniques. Archaeological methods had been rapidly developing during the course of the twentieth century, and Bagatti's methods were those of the first quarter of that century.

Both factors affected Bagatti's work at the Church of the Annunciation. The excavation was conducted, recorded, and published in a style obsolete when it began, let alone when it ended.

Nevertheless, he dug the church well within the limitations of those methods, and recorded and published it in enough detail for it to be reinterpreted in my own work.

Using his records, in the light of later archaeological research, I have been able to reinterpret the sequence of Roman and later activity at the Church of the Annunciation site as follows.

The earliest activity dating from the period of history with which we are concerned here consists of artificial caves, cisterns, and storage pits cut into the rock. (See Figure 2.3.) The pits included examples with three storeys of interconnected artificial voids, presumably to pack as much storage as possible into the available space. This might suggest that space was limited, at least for this purpose—more typical of larger settlements rather than individual farms or the smaller villages.

Several cisterns were also so large as to make it implausible that they were for a single household. These may have been either communal cisterns constructed for several families, or the water supply for a craftworking process.

Some of the caves and cisterns were connected by narrow tunnels cut in the rock. A few had approximately circular scoops—probably to hold jars or other containers—in their floors, ovens, or hearths. There were also agricultural installations belonging to this phase: olive presses, rock-cut basins, and probably a wine press.

Artificial caves, and natural caverns, were often used in this period elsewhere for storerooms, for craftworking areas, stables, and homes. Even today this happens in rural communities elsewhere in the Middle East. As late as the twentieth century there were examples of utilized caves in central Nazareth itself.

Figure 2.3. One of the first-century artificial caves at the Church of the Annunciation site. From *Roman-period and Byzantine Nazareth and its hinterland*, 1st ed., by Ken Dark, copyright 2020 by Imprint; reproduced by permission of Taylor & Francis Group.

That is, what was found at the Church of the Annunciation is less exotic than might be supposed. The evidence of artificial caves cannot be taken to indicate that this was a settlement of cave dwellers. These were probably stables, storage, and working spaces rather than dwellings, but a few may have been used for human occupation.

The presence of such features is, then, best interpreted as evidence for an agricultural settlement. This could have included structures, perhaps stone-built houses, above the underground features, evidence for which has been destroyed by later building on the site. Several lines of cut bedrock could be rock-cut walls or the foundations for built walls on the ancient ground surface. Alternatively, people could have lived in the immediate vicinity and used this area for storage, stables, and the processing of crops.

What is unusual compared to other sites where similar features have been found is the number and distribution of these artificial caves, pits, and agricultural installations. Earlier excavations also found them in the area of the present courtyard between the Church of the Annunciation and nearby St Joseph's church. (See Figure 2.4.) A few, including one large artificial cave linked to a tunnel, were under St Joseph's itself.

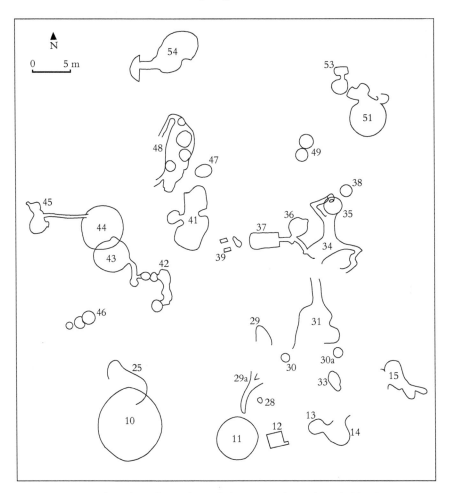

Figure 2.4. Analytical outline plan of the certainly and probably first-century rock-cut spaces at the Church of the Annunciation site. Feature 31 is the Cave of the Annunciation. The narrow tunnels suggesting use as hiding places in the First Jewish Revolt of the AD 60s can clearly be seen. Some outlines overlap because they were cut at different levels. From *Roman-period and Byzantine Nazareth and its hinterland*, 1st ed., by Ken Dark, copyright 2020 by Imprint; reproduced by permission of Taylor & Francis Group.

In all, over sixty rock-cut features have been found in and around the Church of the Annunciation. Most of these may have been used in the Early Roman period, although the quality of dating evidence for them is necessarily variable as some records of earlier excavations were destroyed in World War II.

This evidence suggests that the Church of Annunciation site was part of a substantial Early Roman-period community. It is possible to ascertain more exactly when in the Early Roman period the features belonging to this phase were constructed from the earliest pottery associated with them and from their relationship with the rock-cut tunnels characteristic of the site.

These rock-cut tunnels are clearly later than the agricultural features. Some cut through the walls of rock-cut pits or water cisterns in ways which it would be hard to imagine would have allowed their continued use for their original purpose.

Narrow rock-cut tunnels of this sort are found at other sites. There, they are typical of the hiding places associated with the First Jewish Revolt, which ended in Galilee in AD 70. Such hiding places have a distinctive set of characteristics. These include narrow tunnels of the sort found at the Church of the Annunciation, and locking and blocking devices are also found on the site.

Most of these hiding places reused pre-existing agricultural features, including cisterns, presses, and pits within villages. The rock-cut tunnels connected those underground spaces in a way which made them easy to defend and inaccessible except by crawling into them.

This comparative evidence enables us to date the tunnels. Of course, the agricultural facilities—the caves, presses, pits, and cisterns—would have to be at least of the same date as, or probably earlier than, the tunnels cut into them. As they were plainly used before being reconfigured in this way, we can say that these were constructed before AD 70, possibly much earlier.

Associated objects support this dating. There is a lot of pottery from the Church of the Annunciation site. It includes Late Hellenistic vessels, such as a cosmetic or medical *unguentarium* (small tubular vessel) of a type which can be dated to the second century BC. There is also cooking and storage pottery of types dateable at Sepphoris and other excavated sites to the first century AD.

Among the ceramic lamps found at the site there is at least one northern collar neck lamp dating between the late first century BC and early first century AD. Others may include a type which dates in Galilee from before about 70, as well as possibly Hellenistic types.

Finds of pottery and lamps, therefore, support the interpretation that someone was living at the site in the Late Hellenistic period and early first century AD. There is no archaeological reason to doubt that this site could have been in continuous use from the second century BC until the period of the First Jewish Revolt.

Between the use of the agricultural installations and the tunnels there was an intervening episode when further storage pits were dug. These can be shown to be later than the agricultural features by their relationship with them, but they are also earlier than the tunnels. These phases were all earlier than the construction of large cisterns that are more or less circular in out-line, probably constructed at some point between the late first and fourth centuries.

Among the underground spaces dated to the earliest Roman-period activity is the famous Cave of the Annunciation. The Cave is where many twenty-first-century pilgrims believe that the angel announced to the Virgin Mary that she would give birth to Jesus. This is a long-lasting trad-ition, stretching back to at least the Late Roman period.

Something more can be said on the basis of archaeology about the use of the Cave of the Annunciation in the Early Roman period. It might have originally been a natural cave but, if so, this is obscured by extensive later remodelling. Within the cave, the earliest features currently identifiable may be a semicircular cut in its south-east face and possibly a small hollow in its floor, of the type interpreted elsewhere as the place for a pot or other container.

Like many others, this cave has a tunnel connecting it with another underground space. Four rock-cut pits were probably also parts of the same complex.

This seems to have been an agricultural installation comprising a press and storage facilities. It went through at least one phase of modification before being cut by the tunnel. According to the dating system proposed for those features cut and linked by tunnels it was, therefore, probably in use for some time before AD 70. Pottery and stone vessel fragments found in asso-ciation with this agricultural complex support a first-century date. These include a Late Hellenistic lamp sherd and two limestone vessel fragments.

The Cave of the Annunciation, therefore, actually was probably part of the early first-century settlement. So, in their implied dating of the com-plex, modern and earlier pilgrims and the present Church of the

Annunciation authorities—who consider it to have been in use in the early first century AD—are most likely correct.

Bagatti's excavation also provides evidence for a series of churches at the site, beginning in the fourth century. The first was a small, but elaborately decorated, structure close to the Cave of the Annunciation. It might have been at this time that an artificial cave with unusual features, perhaps indicating its use for veneration of a saint, was constructed next to the Cave, although it may have been a reused cave from an earlier period.

In the fifth century a floor mosaic, with an inscription saying that it was dedicated by Conon, a deacon—member of the Christian clergy—from Jerusalem, was added to the cave-shrine. The name Conon is unusual. Its use here is especially interesting, because it recalls the earlier Conon in the *Martyrdom of Conon*.

The dating means that Conon the martyr and the deacon Conon can't be the same man. There is no reason to assume they were even relatives. But it is possible that the deacon dedicated this floor at Nazareth because the saint was his namesake.

After an intervening phase where the area outside the Cave of the Annunciation was covered by a cobbled surface, and many pottery lamps deposited, a new church was built, probably in the late fifth century. This was very elaborately decorated, including multicoloured mosaic floors, some of which were laid over the others attesting long-lasting patronage, presumably by wealthy Christians. The church was associated with graffiti supporting its identification as the Byzantine Church of the Annunciation, known from written sources. A small monastery was constructed adjacent to it.

The Byzantine church was eventually replaced by an impressive Crusader cathedral after the capture of Nazareth in 1099. This lasted until the eventual Muslim conquest of Nazareth. Throughout the period of Muslim rule, the Cave of the Annunciation continued to be venerated, and a Franciscan church was eventually built for pilgrims in the seventeenth century. The present cathedral-sized basilica is the successor of this church and its subsequent Franciscan replacement in the eighteenth century.

Subsequent archaeological work in Nazareth

Since the Church of the Annunciation excavation ended, almost all archaeological work in Nazareth, except my own and two American research projects, has consisted of IAA rescue excavations and surveys.

IAA rescue excavations cast new light on ancient Nazareth. One of these located a large Roman-period quarry on the steep northern side of Har Nadiv, a steep hill that is today in the city's suburbs. The quarry is important because it shows the same techniques of stoneworking evidenced in the smaller quarries of Nahal Zippori, here in a dated context.

Even more informative was the excavation at Wadi el-Juani, where a Roman-period track led to quarrying and agricultural terraces with semi-circular watchtowers built of unmortared stone, or 'drystone' as it is often called. This confirms the evidence found by the American Nazareth Village project, which identified similar features, along with agricultural presses, closer to the centre of Nazareth.

Between them, these two excavations show that people living in Nazareth probably engaged in the same agricultural and quarrying activities evidenced in the valley. They also provide direct evidence that they were capable of constructing well-made terraces, levelling steep hillsides, and building drystone walls.

Rescue excavations closer to the Church of the Annunciation, both directed by the IAA archaeologist Yardenna Alexandre, have produced fascinating evidence directly related to human occupation in what is today the city centre of Nazareth.

Alexandre excavated two areas in and near Mary's Well. In one—called by her 'Church Square'—in the open paved area in front of the Greek Orthodox church of St Gabriel, she found three wall fragments (of uncertain, but pre-medieval, date) and Late Hellenistic pottery. Hellenistic coins were also found at the site—the only ones so far known from Nazareth—supporting the interpretation of activity of that date in the vicinity of the well. In the other excavation area, which she called 'Fountain Square', there were water channels dating to the Roman period. Coins, pottery, and a ceramic lamp of Roman-period date suggest Roman-period occupation.

However, it is uncertain how this relates to Late Hellenistic and Roman-period Nazareth. Egeria's testimony shows that Mary's Well was outside, although close to, fourth-century Nazareth. Consequently, the occupation at Mary's Well might be evidence for Late Hellenistic and Roman-period occupation in Nazareth, but might be associated with another settlement adjacent to it.

Alexandre's other excavation for the IAA certainly did show Early Roman-period occupation in the centre of modern Nazareth. This took place during the construction of the International Marian Center, and hence is known as the IMC site. Alexandre has produced a good excavation report on the site, and the identification and interpretation of the structures and finds are based on her account of the excavation rather than being my own interpretation, except where indicated.

The excavation found several rooms of a Late Hellenistic and Early Roman-period building. These rooms were largely constructed of stone, but also used rock-cut walls up to 90 centimetres high. Like one of the rock-cut structures in Moshav Zippori, some rooms of the building at the IMC site had floors cut down into the rock surface. Other floors were made of crushed limestone placed directly on top of the natural rock surface.

The walls were usually built of roughly coursed limestone rubble, but they include a wall that incorporated upright slabs with rubble infilling in the gaps between these stones. This last type of construction is rare in Early Roman-period Galilee, but I have seen it in one of the buildings at Yodefat, a large village or small town destroyed in the First Jewish Revolt and apparently deserted thereafter.

A series of superimposed rock-cut storage pits had been dug below some of the floors of the building. These closely resemble those at the Church of the Annunciation site. This resemblance, and the accompanying finds—on which more is said below—support the interpretation of the building as a house.

In view of its relevance to the Sisters of Nazareth site, it is also worth noting that these walls stood as ruins into the medieval period. Then, the walls of a Crusader-period vaulted building were built on them, using the ruinous stubs of earlier walls as foundations.

The Late Hellenistic and Early Roman-period occupation at the IMC site seems to have been continuous. This was accompanied by numerous finds from both periods. The majority of objects were pieces of cooking and storage pots. There were also limestone vessel fragments, and other items of worked stone, metal, and bone.

Cooking pots were typically made of Kefar Hananya ware, hard red pottery made in a Jewish village further north in Galilee. Storage vessels were common in both the Late Hellenistic and Early Roman-period pottery groups at the site. These include Shikhin jars, so called because they were made at the Jewish village of Shikhin just north of Sepphoris. At Sepphoris, they are dated to between the first and late third century AD. Alexandre observes that on her excavation, also for the IAA, at Karm er-Ras they first occur in the first half of the first century AD.

In my survey in the valley I had observed that Kefar Hananya cooking pots and Shikhin storage jars formed the standard 'package' of household pottery (abbreviated by me as 'KHS') in the Nazareth area during the Early Roman period. Consequently, the occurrence of both types at the IMC site strongly supports Alexandre's interpretation that this is an Early Roman-period house.

In addition to the cooking pots and storage jars, sherds of Early Roman knife-pared ('Herodian') lamps were found at the site. This is a type of lamp frequently found in Galilean settlements dated to the Early Roman period. Intriguingly, many of the lamps in Galilee were manufactured in the Jerusalem area. In an Early Roman-period Jewish cultural context, this preference may have been based on the religious significance of Jerusalem rather than simple trading success. The interpretation that the structure was associated with a Jewish cultural context is strengthened by the presence of limestone vessel fragments.

Among the other finds, there were shards of glass from vessels, and a Roman coin of the emperor Claudius dating to AD 50 or 51. Basalt grinding stones—probably for grinding corn to make into bread—must also have been brought to Nazareth, as this type of stone is absent from the local geology.

These objects, and the cooking and storage pottery, may imply that the occupants of the building had sufficient disposable wealth to obtain goods produced elsewhere. This, in turn, suggests a household existing at more than minimum subsistence level.

The only well-dated group of animal bones associated with first-century Nazareth was also recovered from this excavation. Analysis of the bones, by Nimrod Marom for the IAA, showed that they consisted of cattle, sheep/goat (it is difficult for even a specialist to tell the difference between these), chicken, and donkey. The cattle and sheep/goat bones bore butchery marks, showing the use of these animals for food. Conversely, there is no reason to suppose that donkey meat was consumed. Again, the animal bones support the domestic interpretation of the Early Roman-period structures.

A loom weight, used in weaving cloth, also supports a domestic interpretation of the site. Its pyramidal form is well paralleled at other Galilean Early Roman-period settlements. However, pyramidal loom weights appear to go out of use in Galilee after the end of the first century. So, this is yet more evidence for the IMC structure being a first-century house.

Evidence for first-century Nazareth

This overview of the existing sources of evidence for the first-century settlement at Nazareth shows that there is sufficient written and archaeological evidence to confirm that there was certainly a settlement of this date in the centre of modern Nazareth. Archaeology shows that the origins of this settlement lay in the Late Hellenistic period. (See Figure 2.5.)

There is also evidence for continuity between the first-century settlement and its fourth-century counterpart. Unless the fourth-century inhabitants of Nazareth were ignorant of the name of their settlement in earlier generations, it seems reasonable to assume on this basis that the fourth-century settlement stood on approximately the same site as its first-century counterpart.

That is, the first-century settlement we can see through archaeology in the centre of modern Nazareth is the Nazareth referred to in the Gospels. This raises the question of what can be reliably said about this settlement from written sources other than the Gospel accounts.

Written sources, except for the brief mentions in the Gospels, are unhelpful in reconstructing the first-century settlement. To gain more information about first-century Nazareth as a place it is, therefore, necessary to use archaeological evidence, along with an understanding of its ancient topographical context and natural environment.

As shown in this chapter, there may be limited archaeological evidence for first-century Nazareth, but there is some. In fact, a consistent picture can be built up of agricultural terraces, of rock-cut tombs, of quarries, and of agricultural installations such as olive and wine presses and storage places. As we shall see, the IMC site and Sisters of Nazareth site also offer a largely consistent impression of the houses of first-century Nazareth.

In this way, archaeology gives us a greater understanding of what this settlement was like and of life within it. This brings us to the Sisters of Nazareth site. In the next chapter we shall find out how it was discovered and why—even apart from its possible implications for first-century Nazareth—the first archaeological work on the site was pioneering in the worldwide development of archaeology.

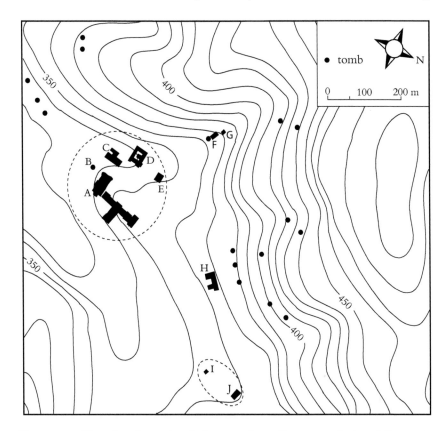

Figure 2.5. Plan showing what is known about Roman-period and Byzantine Nazareth from archaeology. Numbers = contours indicated in metres. Dots = rock-cut tombs. A= Church of the Annunciation site, with its main buildings in black. B = Roman-period rock-cut tomb. C = Franciscan Casa Nova hostel. D = Sisters of Nazareth convent. Roman-period tombs are located approximately. E = 'Synagogue Church'. F = Maronite church. G = Mensa Christi (Mensa church). H = Orthodox Christian episcopal building, with undated artificial caves. I = present Mary's Well. J = Church of St Gabriel (the Orthodox Church of the Annunciation). Dashed lines indicate outer limits of the areas in which Roman period and/or pottery have been found—probably the minimum extent of Roman-period settlement. The wadi ran north-east to north-west, to the north of the Church of the Annunciation, below the Casa Nova hostel and towards Mary's Well. From *Roman-period and Byzantine Nazareth and its hinterland*, 1st ed., by Ken Dark, copyright 2020 by Imprint; reproduced by permission of Taylor & Francis Group.

3

Amazing discoveries

Mère Marie Giraud, convent superior and pioneering archaeologist

On Christmas Eve 1881, the Sisters of Nazareth acquired the present convent site. One of the first things they did, presumably after celebrating Christmas, was to repair an underground cistern, that is, a storage tank for water. This cistern, like many others in Nazareth cut into the natural limestone, was used by the nineteenth-century houses which had been on part of the land before the nuns bought it.

The nuns hired a local workman to carry out the repairs. Digging down to get at the cistern, the workman came across an almost complete granite column over 3 metres long. This was obviously from an ancient building of some size—quite unlike the houses then on the site. The column caught the attention of the convent superior, Mère Marie Giraud (1840–1900), who noted it in her diary.

The next year, workmen constructing the convent's east enclosure wall discovered large stone building blocks and several pieces of sculpted stone. Late that year, fragments of another column were found in the north-west of the convent garden. This confirmed it: plainly, at least one much earlier building had stood on the convent site. Judging from the sculpted stone and columns, it was more than an ordinary house.

Mère Giraud knew that sculpted stone and columns could indicate a church dating from the Byzantine or Crusader period. Perhaps earlier Christians had worshipped at the convent site. This brought to mind a conversation which she had when the convent bought the land.

A local woman said that it was once the site of the 'tomb of the saint', a 'just man', where a 'great church' had stood. Two people are called 'Just' in

Figure 3.1. The cross-vaulted room, looking south. Photo: Ken Dark.

the Bible: St Joseph and the St James described in the Gospels as the brother of Jesus. Both of them had lived in Nazareth, of course, but James was reputed to be buried in Jerusalem.

Mère Giraud wasn't a gullible person. All sorts of legends circulated in the nineteenth-century Holy Land—but perhaps, she wondered, the woman really knew something about this place. Could it have been a Byzantine or Crusader church? What about the burial place of St Joseph? He had to be buried somewhere!

Then, on 18 October 1884, further work on the convent found a stone-built room, covered with a cross-vault, about 5 metres below the surface. (See Figure 3.1.) Was this evidence of the suspected church? Mère Giraud felt that the nuns had to investigate it.

When they dug further down, the nuns found that the room was filled to within 10–20 centimetres of its ceiling with compact clay. This clay eventually turned out to be a 2.3-metre alluvial deposit. An alluvial deposit is one deriving from sedimentation by water. In this instance it was apparently due to soil washed in by rain coming through the opening at the top of the room.

The room survives today, and must have been an impressive discovery when first exposed.

It was at this point that Mère Giraud made the momentous decision to undertake more excavations. But rather than call in an outside expert (even then there were 'biblical archaeologists' in the Holy Land), she decided that the nuns would continue the excavation, directing it herself.

Mère Giraud's workforce was comprised of the other nuns who, although assisted by workmen, did much of the actual digging themselves. One workman, interviewed as an old man, recalled seeing Mère Giraud constantly monitoring the work, clutching her characteristic little notebook for recording what had been found.

This was among the earliest archaeological projects anywhere in the world initiated and directed by a woman. What is more, Mère Giraud was succeeded in this role by the superiors of the convent up to the 1930s. Digging nuns must have been a regular sight at the convent in the decades either side of 1900.

This was also the first archaeological excavation in central Nazareth. As mentioned in Chapter 2, Prosper Viaud and Benedict Vlaminck began digging at the Church of the Annunciation only about eight years later. Mère Giraud wasn't only a pioneer of women in archaeology; she also began the archaeological study of Nazareth.

Mère Giraud's excavation of the cross-vaulted room proved remarkably productive. In the clay the nuns found fragments of marble showing chisel marks, column fragments, Byzantine coins, pieces of pottery lamps, and even a complete lamp. This confirmed Mère Giraud's initial impression that the earlier discoveries indicated Byzantine or earlier activity at the site. It was beginning to get exciting, especially in the sedate world of a nineteenth-century French convent.

At the bottom of the walls, a heap of mosaic cubes (which archaeologists call *tesserae*)—coloured green, blue, gold, red, and pink—was piled on the floor. These had probably fallen from elaborate mosaics on the walls of the room. It was obviously more than just another cistern. Was it part of the 'great church'?

Excited by their discoveries, Mère Giraud led the nuns to explore further underground spaces leading off from the cross-vaulted room. They followed the same route along which I had been led on my first visit to the convent in 2005. But for them it was much harder going—every part of the underground spaces was full of soil.

The earth had to be dug out and removed from what continued to be a very restricted working area. In the 1880s, anyone getting into the cross-vaulted room had to clamber through a hole in the roof. They must have taken the soil out that way also.

Moreover, the nuns were digging by clearing away the earth to form tunnels—sideways rather than from the top. Sudden collapse of either the soil into which they dug or the earlier structures was a real danger. Doing all of this in nineteenth-century nuns' habits must have made it even harder.

Then there was the question of light. Even today, with much more of the underground space open, when the electric lighting is turned off it is dark in the Cellar. Then, there must have been few sources of light other than the small opening in the ceiling of the cistern, candles carried by the nuns, and any lanterns the nuns or their workmen brought with them.

Consequently, this was dark, cramped, dusty, and dangerous work. At times it must have been more like mining than ordinary archaeological excavation. That no accidents or injuries involving people are mentioned at all is itself testimony to the nuns' care and caution.

Progress was necessarily slow. Finding so many objects—the convent diaries and other contemporary descriptions are full of them—must have made it even slower. The soil had to be sorted and fragile items handled with care.

Nonetheless, Mère Giraud made meticulous records of what she found. Some exist today. They are less detailed than those of a twenty-first-century archaeological project, of course, but they give a very good indication of what the nuns found.

Mère Giraud was also good at interpreting her discoveries. There are no flights of fancy, but logical inferences from the structures and objects found. It was a remarkable achievement for someone who was untrained in archaeology and at the same time both running a convent and undertaking the religious duties of a nun.

Digging their way forward with pickaxes, the nuns first came to the flight of steps leading down into the Large Cave. They were amazed to find such a big underground space right below their convent.

Here, they discovered a thick layer of ash under the alluvial clay, including a charred pottery lamp which later research would show is crucial for dating the end of the medieval use of the site. First, they dug along the east side of the cave, then turned their attention to the western half.

Exploring the Large Cave

Like the cross-vaulted room, the cave turned out to be full of archaeological interest. Along one side of its curved end there was a flat-topped bench cut into the rock, with four rectangular basins cut into its surface. The basins had small holes in their sides so that liquid could drain from one to another.

The basins had probably once been lined with lead, of which traces remained within them. There were small circular holes, probably for a lead pipe, in the rock face of the cave immediately above the south of the basins. Three other smaller basins—which were constructed out of mortared stone, rather than cut into the rock—continued the line of four rock-cut basins southward.

These smaller basins fed into one another from south to north, just like the rock-cut basins. The nuns found a grave, also cut into the rock, beneath the smaller basins. This grave contained the crouched skeleton of a man wearing a ring, probably made of copper alloy. (See Figure 3.2.)

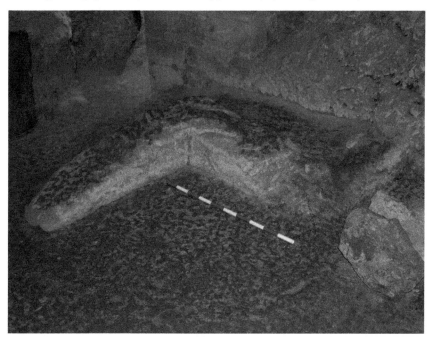

Figure 3.2. The 'Bishop's Tomb', actually the cut-down remnant of Tomb 2 in which the nuns found a skeleton misidentified by them as that of a bishop because of a ring on its finger. Photo: Ken Dark.

The ring led the nuns to suppose that the grave might be that of a Byzantine bishop. A ring is one of the symbols of a bishop, and they thought that this was a Byzantine church site.

We shall see later that the grave is more likely to have been a Roman-period Jewish burial. But even today it is sometimes called 'the bishop's grave'. The nineteenth-century nuns reburied the skeleton, although there is no record of where they did so.

The nuns continued to dig in the cave and adjacent rock-cut rooms to its east, which they recognized as water-storage cisterns. The largest of these is that visible today through an opening from the vaulted room. The clay filling of this cistern formed three thick layers.

In the bottom layer they found pottery vessels and lamps and small glass phials probably used for perfume (called by archaeologists *unguentaria*). Remarkably, there were also well-preserved fragments of gold-embroidered cloth in the next layer, along with painted pottery and ash. The cloth, which was later lost, was probably preserved by the clay around it sealing it from the air which would otherwise have caused its decay. The top layer of clay contained what was described as a mixture of objects, although what these were was either unrecorded or that record has been lost.

In the 1880s, archaeologists were only just paying attention to the build-up of layers on sites, so in this way the nuns were at the forefront of excavation techniques. Indeed, although again unrealized until my work, the glass phials found in this cistern offer the first recorded archaeological evidence for an early first-century settlement in Nazareth.

Unlike many of the nuns' finds, the glass phials survive in the convent museum today. Some of them can be accurately dated by comparison with examples of known date found elsewhere. Most of them are made of green glass. At least two fragments of pear-shaped vessels are characteristic of the first century AD. There are also ten fragments (shards) of others made in dark-blue glass with yellow glass trails, which date somewhere between the first century BC and the first century AD.

Glass phials such as these were either put in rock-cut tombs or used for perfume in houses. The only way in which these vessels could get into the rock-cut cistern at this date was by falling through the opening at its top or being used within it. The top of the hill would be a very unlikely spot for a rock-cut tomb, as these were usually cut into hillsides, but as these came from a cistern rather than a tomb they probably were washed in from the hilltop.

This evidence suggests that wherever the first-century settlement at Nazareth was, it included what is today the nuns' back garden. It also suggests that this cistern was originally used as part of that first-century settlement. These finds were the first to show what would today be recognized by archaeologists as material evidence for early first-century occupation at Nazareth. This is a discovery which should be attributed to Mère Giraud rather than any later archaeologist.

Back to the nuns' excavation. North of the cistern containing the glass phials the nuns found a rock-cut room. This was approximately rectangular and covered by a medieval barrel vault, an arched ceiling resembling half a barrel in shape. A carved limestone water conduit with a U-shaped cross section, high in its wall, led into the cistern from yet another rock-cut cistern to its north. On its west side there was a rock-cut doorway with a rounded, but irregular, shape leading down rock-cut steps into the Large Cave.

The series of rooms on the east side of the cave, therefore, comprised two cisterns either side of the rectangular room. The curved end of the Large Cave had probably also originally been another cistern of similar date, access to which was through a hole in its ceiling. This opening was later used as a 'light well', intended to allow daylight into the cave. (See Figure 3.3.)

The rectangular room itself had an entrance to the Large Cave, and a doorway, leading to a blocked passage, was positioned high in the west wall of the rectangular room. There is no record that the passage behind it was ever explored by the nuns or any later investigator of the site. Even today, its blocking remains unopened.

Meanwhile, there was drama in the Large Cave. On 1 April 1886, Mère Giraud began to dig in the north-west part of the cave. She was looking for a well on the advice of 'a German engineer'—probably Gottlieb Schumacher, who, in 1889, wrote one of the few serious academic papers published about the site before 2006. Mère Giraud's excavation found another rock-cut cistern, but suddenly there was an explosion! It had hit a pocket of methane.

No one was hurt, but understandably excavation in that area ceased. Nevertheless, after a few months break, Mère Giraud began digging again at the other end of the Large Cave on 29 September 1886. She wasn't going to let a little explosion put her off.

Immediately, the nuns found a high wall facing the entrance to the Large Cave from the cross-vaulted room. This wall was built on an alluvial deposit like the one which had filled both the cross-vaulted room and the cave.

Figure 3.3. The 'light well' in the Large Cave, probably formed out of the opening of an Early Roman-period cistern. Photo: Ken Dark.

The wall had a series of shallow niches along its top, and clear evidence of an association with water. There was a stone-carved channel for water, like the one in the rectangular room next to the cave. A built cistern behind the wall fed into the stone basins at the other end of the cave. What exactly it was used for is unknown, but it added to the evidence that the cave was connected with the collection and use of water.

In February 1887, the nuns broke through the wall—apparently on its north side, because its east face remains intact—and found two rock-cut burial slots behind it. These contained illegible, but seemingly ancient, coins. Two similar burial slots were found in the south side of the cave, also containing coins. There were now five rock-cut graves in the south and centre of the cave: these four, and the one (the so-called 'bishop's grave') with the crouched skeleton and ring.

At least four of these graves were in the sort of burial slots often called *loculi* in Mediterranean archaeology. (See Figure 3.4.) *Loculi* are common in the rock-cut Roman-period Jewish tombs of the Holy Land, of which

Figure 3.4. Roman-period *loculi* from Tomb 2 deliberately conserved and decorated with mosaic in the later cave-church. Photo: Ken Dark.

thousands are known today. Even in the 1880s they were recognizable features associated with Jewish burial in the Roman Empire.

From March to October that year the nuns took another break from excavation. Then they began again at the end of November, digging the floor of the cave down to the natural rock. In the course of this excavation, another four small basins were found on the surface of the alluvial clay next to the wall with the niches. This again reinforced the connection between this wall and the Large Cave, with water.

The cistern behind the wall fed into these basins and those at the other end of the cave. Mère Giraud realized that this suggested a functional connection between the wall and the basins in the curved end of the cave. This meant, she reasoned, that use of the two sets of basins was also, at least partially, of the same date.

None of the earlier investigators of the site seem to have realized this, but this evidence seems to me to mean that there must be at least two alluvial deposits in the cave: one under the niched wall and its associated features; the other filling the Large Cave, the cisterns to its east and the vaulted room, almost to their ceilings. Without Mère Giraud's careful notes, this crucial fact would have gone unrecorded.

However, at the time Mère Giraud was more concerned with the many objects and sculpted stones turning up throughout the excavation. She recorded fragments of stone columns under the arched entrance to the north of the cave, fragments of imported marble, and a large fragment of a stone screen. Pottery, shards of glass vessels, coins, and metal objects were also found.

There were stone cubes from mosaics in many colours—green, yellow, red, and pink. Some were made of glass covered in gold leaf. The mosaic cubes were found in the whole length of the Large Cave, sometimes in heaps, and in the cross-vaulted room. There was also a lot of lime plaster in the cave, which could have been used to create a smooth surface for mosaics on its uneven walls.

Mère Giraud herself realized that many of these mosaic cubes had probably fallen from the walls of the cave. However, one of her drawings of the excavation shows a panel of mosaic decorated with an equal-armed cross with dots between each of its arms. This was probably from a mosaic floor.

It was at this point that Schumacher, the engineer whose advice seems to have led to the explosion in 1886, published a brief description of his visit to the site in July 1888. This was just after the nuns had stopped digging in the Large Cave.

Schumacher confirms what Giraud recorded and mentions 'signs of an original plastering in different parts' on the walls and 'piles of good thick mortar-cover'. Schumacher also describes a small room on the south-west of the cave containing another cistern. From his published plan—which is very schematic—there seems to have been another, empty grave in this small room.

Schumacher notes that the nuns had found a lot of pottery 'painted with simple black stripes'. This was probably what archaeologists today would call medieval Handmade Geometrically Painted Ware (HMGPW). Other pottery vessels and lamps, glass beads, and Roman, Byzantine, and medieval Islamic coins were also mentioned by Schumacher. These finds back up the nuns' own records of Roman-period, Byzantine, and medieval objects.

Schumacher drew some of the objects found in the cave: a stylized bone figurine of a woman, a well-carved limestone statuette of a robed figure with one sleeved arm across the waist and what appears to be a stole or sash, and a small marble column. He also drew one of the complete lamps, which is easily recognizable as a Crusader type from the end of the twelfth century or turn of the thirteenth. This lamp, he says, was found in a deep ash deposit at the north end of the cave.

Both the bone figurine and the lamp are preserved today in the convent museum. Both give important clues to the dating of the Large Cave.

To begin with the figurine. This is a flat, elongated piece of bone, rounded on the edges and inscribed in a mixture of lines and 'ring and dot' design, showing what is plainly meant to be a female figure. It is a type of object known elsewhere on sites occupied in the early Islamic period. However, these figurines were probably produced by Christian, rather than Muslim, communities. As a group of objects these figurines can be dated to between the seventh and eleventh centuries. Very stylized examples, such as the one at the Sisters of Nazareth site, seem to date specifically to between the eighth and eleventh centuries. There has been some academic debate over their function, for example whether they were dolls or had another purpose. A strong possibility is that they were associated with Christian pilgrimage, being placed at shrines in thanks for a cure.

Obviously, an eighth- to eleventh-century object in the cave suggests that it might have been in use in that period. Likewise, if the figurines were associated with places of Christian pilgrimage, then it might imply such pilgrimage to the Sisters of Nazareth site. How it came to be in the cave will be discussed later in the chapter. But first it is worth considering the lamp. (See Figure 3.5.)

The deep ash deposit in which the lamp was found is present throughout the Large Cave. It almost certainly represents a major fire, which ended the use of the cave until after the nuns had excavated it. Things could have been dropped into the cave later, through the opening in its roof, but until the nineteenth-century excavation no one could have stood up inside the cave after the ash had been deposited.

Because the pottery lamp was found in the ash, its date provides a *terminus post quem* for when the ash was deposited. The lamp is of a type called by archaeologists 'Slipper Lamps'. These were made during the Crusader period and this specific type is dated more specifically from the late twelfth century until around 1200.

The world expert on Crusader pottery in the Holy Land, Dr Edna Stern—who wrote the standard book on its dating—examined the lamp

Figure 3.5. The Crusader lamp, dating to the late twelfth or very early thirteenth century, found by the nineteenth-century nuns in an ash deposit filling the Large Cave. This provides crucial dating evidence suggesting that the ash derives from the deliberate burning of the Crusader church in 1187. Photo: Ken Dark.

with me in 2008 and confirmed the type and date of the object. Consequently, the ash layer in the Large Cave must date to the late twelfth century or later.

As the nuns' later discoveries show, this ash layer forms part of a major episode of destruction by fire affecting the whole area within the convent. Although it could theoretically have been the consequence of an accidental fire, the most plausible context—given the date of the lamp—is the destruction of Nazareth in 1187.

Excavating on the surface

Prompted by these underground explorations, Mère Giraud wanted to know what stood above the Large Cave. She excavated in the convent's

Figure 3.6. The rock-cut door leading from the Large Cave to the cisterns and room to its east. Photo: Ken Dark.

back garden. Whether she expected this isn't recorded, but digging here proved to be an even more daunting task. The archaeological deposits were more than 5 metres deep in places.

Excavating almost the entire garden, the nuns found the ruins of a rectangular building on an east–west alignment. This measured 17 metres long by 8 metres wide and had a curved eastern end resembling the apse of a church.

Near the centre of the north wall of the building there were three arched openings into which water had been led through an underground stone-lined tunnel. This tunnel, or conduit, led to the 'Synagogue Church', a standing medieval building uphill from the convent in the present street market area. The conduit is the only evidence for a water source at the 'Synagogue Church', although its site has never been extensively excavated.

The next event was to play a crucial part in the history of archaeological investigation at the convent. The famous biblical scholar Victor Guérin visited the site in 1888 and suggested—as mentioned in Chapter 1—that it might be the 'Church of the Nutrition', described in the seventh-century pilgrim account called *De Locis Sanctis*. Unsurprisingly, this suggestion excited the nuns, who began to wonder if that was what they had found.

Newly motivated, the nuns dug southwards from the cross-vaulted room. Work had to pause while construction took place to prevent the room and Large Cave from collapsing. It was underground that their next important discoveries were made.

The nuns had been working for six years to clear a way through a stone-lined passageway linking the cross-vaulted room with the area to its south (Figs. 3.7–3.12). Then, on 21 September 1898, they discovered a room to its west: the Chambre Obscure. They found that it was covered by a vault and had a window-like opening in its south-east wall. It was through that opening that the nuns first saw another, much larger, barrel-vaulted room containing the remains of what they subsequently called 'the house'.

Again, disaster struck. The vault over 'the house' collapsed in a storm before they could get inside it. Looking for a way into the collapsed vaulted area, they found that the rest of the passageway leading south was blocked by a very solid wall. Even beyond the wall, they needed to dig out more soil in order to progress. It was painfully slow work.

The first thing to appear as the soil was removed was a flight of stairs built of mortared stone. Beyond this they found a well-built stone wall.

Figure 3.7. The 'well' in the cross-vaulted room, actually a place for taking water up out of a large deep cistern on the other side of the wall. Photo: Ken Dark.

Working along this wall they saw that another wall south from it had once incorporated two Crusader-style arches. The nuns quickly dismantled the only standing arch for fear that it might fall on them. They had probably had enough of sudden collapses.

Then they dug in the opposite direction, to the east, and found another similar stairway. At its base were the fallen remains of what was described as a landing. As Mère Giraud realized, this had presumably once connected the two stairways at an upper level. Having cleared the area immediately south and west of the entrance of the passageway leading south of the Chambre Obscure, they began to work yet further south.

In this area, stone paving covered the floor. The paving was buried below an ash layer. It must have reminded them, rightly as it turned out, of the ash layer in the Large Cave. This ash layer stopped at a substantial east–west mortared stone wall, the western part of which had once supported the vault which had fallen in the storm.

Using their usual method, they dug along the east–west wall. This would trace its course and take them to the west part of the once vaulted area. At

Figure 3.8. The passage leading south from the cross-vaulted room. The entrance from the cross-vaulted room to the passage had been deliberately blocked by a wall when the nuns first discovered it, suggesting that the Crusaders wanted to hide something to its south during the siege of 1187. Photo: Ken Dark.

the bottom of the wall there was a hoard (said to be hundreds) of corroded bronze Crusader coins.

This was the last of Mère Giraud's discoveries in the area that is today in the Cellar. She had found the cross-vaulted room, Large Cave and its adjacent cisterns, the passageway leading to the south, the Chambre Obscure, the stairways and—although she had been unable to reach it—'the house'. This must have far exceeded her expectations when she embarked on her programme of investigating the site about fifteen years earlier.

The new superior, Mère Marie Fancy (1855–1927), whose surname is misrecorded in some reports in the convent archive as Fanay, continued the excavation in summer 1900. Almost immediately an astonishing discovery was made. Mère Fancy herself was digging where the coin hoard had been found—the convent superiors evidently took part in the process of

Figure 3.9. The south of the present Cellar. The area which the nuns discovered when they dug through the blocked passage leading south from the cross-vaulted room. The massive medieval wall, M4, is in the middle distance, with the modern Cellar walls behind. To the left, just in front of Wall M4, is the grille through which the nuns first reached the Crusader chapel beside Tomb 1. Photo: Ken Dark.

excavation—when she came across a heavy square slab placed flat on the ground.

It took two workmen to lift the slab, and underneath it was another slab set into a recess. The workmen found a square opening under the second stone. There was a big empty space below it.

Mère Fancy's workmen refused to enter. They looked scared. From the void came a smell which the nuns likened to incense—a smell which they, of course, knew well from church. The smell lingered for days.

The convent superior was undeterred. She sent two of her slimmest nuns down a ladder through the narrow opening. Looking at the opening today it seems impossible that anyone could get through it. Through the opening was a roughly dome-shaped room, carved into the rock, with what the nuns realized at once was a Christian altar built of slabs on its south.

Figure 3.10. The Crusader chapel next to Tomb 1. Medieval knights' spurs were found on its walls when first discovered by the nuns, along with traces suggesting that it had been hastily abandoned—presumably immediately before the entrances to the tomb and to the passage leading south from the cross-vaulted room were blocked. Photo: Ken Dark.

Pottery lamps, a small chain, and a carved stone stood on the altar, where they had lain since the last time they were used, centuries earlier. The absence of other religious objects, such as a cross or communion chalice, and the abandoned chain—which looked as if it should be attached to another object—hinted that whoever was last using the altar had left in a hurry, snatching things up.

Two iron spurs hung on the wall, probably dedicated in thanks for being delivered from danger. The nuns thought that the spurs belonged to a Crusader knight—and they were probably correct. These, the altar, and the other objects on it left no one in any doubt that they had found a Crusader chapel.

Two blocked openings could be seen in the west of the chapel. Taking out the blocking stones, the nuns entered what they knew to be a rock-cut

Figure 3.11. Roman-period *loculi* from Tomb 1. Unlike Tomb 2, no Roman-period finds at all are recorded from the tomb. Was this because they were already taken away as religious relics in either the Byzantine or Crusader period, or was the tomb never used? Photo: Ken Dark.

Jewish tomb of the type used in the Roman period. No human remains were found in the tomb, but there is no doubt of its date and interpretation.

There had once been an opening on the south of the main chamber of this tomb, but it was also blocked with stones. Removing the stones, the nuns found themselves staring at the back of a millstone-sized stone disc blocking the way forward.

No matter how hard they tried, the nuns were unable to move the heavy stone from within the tomb. It would have been impossible to get a grip on its rim. Mère Fancy decided to dig down from the ground surface above it instead.

About 7 metres below the surface, they arrived at the front of the stone disc. The tomb and stone disc survive today and are in a roughly rectangular cutting out of the rock. This sort of cut is a typical feature of Jewish Roman-period rock-cut tombs and served as a forecourt for the tomb itself.

Figure 3.12. A general view of the south of Structure 1 ('the house'), showing its walls, the remnants of the large medieval vault which once covered it—the scale (left of centre) is positioned to show the line of the vault—and the heavy medieval paving on its south side. The modern walls of the Cellar can be seen in the background. This was the vault which collapsed in heavy rain after the nuns had looked into it and first seen Structure 1 ('the house'). Photo: Ken Dark.

In the soil outside the tomb there were many mosaic cubes. These had presumably fallen from the front of the tomb itself, or from a later building above it. From this side it was possible to roll back the stone and enter through the low rock-cut door of the tomb—rather than clambering through the hole in the ceiling of the adjacent chapel—for the first time in centuries.

The nuns then dug on the ground surface on which they had found the opening through which they first saw the chapel with the altar and hanging spurs. Proceeding first to the west, and then north again, they dug away the rubble from the vault which had collapsed in the storm. It is uncertain from their records whether they were digging underground at this point, or widening their vertical excavation to include this area.

Anyway, digging away the rubble of the collapsed vault exposed the walls of two rooms in what was later called 'the house'. These had floors at different levels and were separated by an east–west stone-built wall. The wall had been constructed at the meeting point of the two Crusader arches which they had found earlier.

There was another, lower, L-shaped stone-built wall in the north-west corner of the northernmost room, and a blocked doorway opened from that room into the Chambre Obscure. They cannot have helped noticing that so many of the entrances in this part of the site had been deliberately blocked—both doors south from the Chambre Obscure and the entrances to the tomb. This suggested that whoever did so had something to hide, and this involved the rooms which they had just found and the tomb itself.

Much of the structure of the two rooms which the nuns had found survives today. But there have also been significant alterations. The approximately east–west wall dividing the two rooms was built of small stones and was completely dug away. The room on the north had a lower floor, the last traces of which were destroyed in 1964. That on the south was a platform of solid paving, but half of this was removed in 1900, when a building with foundation trenches 4 to 7 metres deep was built to protect this part of the site.

The rest of the floor was raised and then relaid at about 15 centimetres higher, accentuating the difference in height between it and the floor immediately to its north. That is, no part of the floor found by the nuns remains intact in its original place today.

Further damage was done to this part of the site in 1900. Today, a wide cut through a massive mortared stone wall—later termed 'M4'—along the south of the structure gives the appearance of two lengths of wall separated by an entrance. In fact, wall M4 had been a continuous east–west barrier transecting the south of this part of the Cellar, but the nuns dug through its centre.

Meanwhile, premodern structures and stonework had begun to be found all around the western and southern sides of the block of land on which the present convent is located. These were even found under the streets running along those sides of the convent.

In 1889, the nuns had decided to build a vaulted classroom for their school in the south-east of the convent. Construction was delayed by problems in obtaining official permission from the authorities, but once these bureaucratic hurdles had been overcome, building finally began in 1891.

Almost at once Mr Salim, the construction foreman, noticed ancient columns, a column capital, and other worked stone in one of the trenches dug along the street running past the front door of the convent. Further inspection revealed a rectangular slab, which the nuns thought was the top of an altar. Then, another column capital and walls were found in the same trench.

This looked like the remains of a building; if the nuns were right about the altar slab, maybe even an ancient church.

Then, to the west, a 4.5-metre-deep trench found what the nuns thought was the outside of a doorway, with what seemed to be another, lower doorway between 3 and 4 metres to its south-east. This was again roughly parallel with the front of the convent, where it faced the street.

Mère Giraud, who was still the superior in 1891, had a 6-metre-long tunnel built to reach these two doorways from within the convent. In the course of my own early twenty-first-century work, with colleagues I entered the disused and very dark tunnel. Clambering into the tunnel from a vertical, stone-lined shaft, we held torches made of rolls of burning paper both for light and to ward off rats and other animals. Searching the whole length of the tunnel, no archaeological features—or wildlife—could be seen within it.

Further excavations by the nuns took place in 1892, again under the direction of Mère Giraud. The first was near the corner of the north–south street bordering the Anglican church, Christ Church. This sits at the end of the little street leading past the front of the convent even today.

The church, a remarkable survival of British involvement in Nazareth, has the appearance inside and out of a Victorian English parish church. It remains very active and an important centre for Nazareth's small but vigorous local Anglican community. The excavation found a short, but solid, wall, later traced further to the north. More of this wall was traced to the north during public works on the street in 1941.

The second excavation in 1892 was just outside the convent parlour. This discovered a substantial arch, but no other information about it seems to survive. Further excavations on the west of the convent were undertaken a little later, in 1895, when a series of cisterns were found deep under what is today the western side of the convent site. These cisterns seem to be associated with a range of approximately rectangular rooms, bordering the east of the present north–south street.

The arches, sculpted stonework, and mortared stone walls of these discoveries suggested to the nuns that they represented Byzantine or medieval buildings. Nothing about them suggests an earlier date. But if they were

Byzantine or medieval, then the fact that they were present all around the perimeter of the convent is itself a surprise. Nothing of those dates was previously known to have existed there.

However, the most spectacular discoveries to come from the nuns' surface excavations were within the convent itself. During construction work on the east of the convent, builders came upon three curved walls forming semicircles or apses (which the nuns called A1, A2, and A3). All of these were built of well-cut blocks of smoothed limestone, about 1 metre long by 60 centimetres wide and 30 centimetres thick. When originally exposed, they were depicted on two measured plans, dated 1900 and 1913, probably drawn by the architect involved in the construction of the convent's present church.

All three apses survived to three or more courses high, and there were traces of mosaic on the inside surface of the walls of at least one of them (A1). An anonymous drawing, said to be based on a lost photograph, shows them standing even higher. However, this seems to depict a partial reconstruction—probably in the original photograph—rather than the state of the apses as found. Another anonymous drawing, probably by a different artist, shows a round-headed arch to the west of the southernmost apse (A1).

The structure incorporating the apses must have been built on a substantial artificial terrace, because the natural contours of the rock fell away sharply below them. The steep sides of the wadi (seasonal riverbed) running through the centre of Nazareth probably explain this sudden drop in the underlying rock surface. That anyone would build such a big building in such a difficult spot might imply that they had a compelling motivation to do so.

The nuns knew that apses could mean that the building was a church. Most church buildings end in one or more apses. They must have wondered if this was the 'great church' of which they had been told when they first bought the convent site.

When the convent church was begun in October 1912, more evidence was found of earlier buildings. A column still in its base, a marble cornice decorated with carved acanthus leaves, a small vault, and bronze coins were all found in the area of the present stairway down to the Cellar outside the convent museum. This placed elaborate ancient surface-built structures right next to the underground components of the site such as the Large Cave.

Then, 4 metres deep, the nuns found a layer of red soil—probably burnt clay (clay often goes red when subjected to burning)—and ash containing what they identified as burnt linen.

Next, the nuns discovered the foundations of solid blocks of mortared stone designed to hold up a building—what architects and archaeologists call 'piers' (P6 and P8). These were accompanied by the fallen components of an arch which those piers had once supported, a burnt marble bowl, and a column base. The piers were cut into a layer containing human bone, perhaps an earlier cemetery.

When the belfry for the new church was being built just to the east of this in March 1913, finds included what may have been a sarcophagus, mosaic cubes, and pieces of marble—some of which were plainly from an elaborate building. As work progressed westward, a column base and a marble bowl decorated with a carving of grapes were also found. A small column was decorated with carvings of acanthus leaves and a cross.

The style of all this stonework was Byzantine and medieval. Of course, this struck the nuns as similar in date to their discoveries in the Large Cave. The cross-decorated column also seemed to confirm their interpretation that there was a Christian building on the site.

On the other side of the convent, there were more discoveries in 1913. These included walls of double thickness infilled with small stones, a small barrel-vaulted structure, a column in its base, and another sculpted architectural fragment. A layer containing ash, human bones, and what the nuns identified as 'linen clothes' was found at a depth of 4 metres. This was, of course, similar to the burnt layer which they had found earlier, and again was associated with a dark red colour, which the nuns thought was dried blood, but was probably actually heavily burnt clay.

The same deposit is also said to have been found 5 metres further south of the area outside the steps which today lead to the south of the convent church, but there it also contained many mosaic cubes. This combination of ash and mosaic cubes was then found at each of the locations selected for the pillars of the new convent cloister.

Putting all this together, as the nuns realized, it seems inescapable that there were one or more major stone buildings, decorated with multicoloured mosaics and held up by stone columns with carved capitals—which had been destroyed by fire. Again, judging from the style of the carved stone, the building or buildings contained both Byzantine and medieval sculpted stone.

Underneath the east side of the site, the rock surface was between 9.5 and 10.5 metres below early twentieth-century ground level. This could be explained by the building sitting on the substantial artificial terrace which, as we have seen, would have been needed to stabilize the ground in this location in order to construct a major building.

Further evidence for the terrace comes from another discovery by the nuns. In 1913, they found a thick north–south wall in the area later used for the chancel of the convent church. Where the west wall of the present convent is located, there was another substantial wall, suggesting a rectangular, or approximately rectangular, platform supporting the building represented by the apses, columns, column capitals, arches, vaults, and mortared stone walls.

This suggests that the Byzantine and medieval building evidenced by these discoveries was almost exactly the size of the whole of the present convent. That would, of course, make it a very big building.

But what sort of building? As the nuns realized, the apses and some of the architectural stonework suggested an answer. Multiple eastern apses are strongly associated in Byzantine architecture with churches, and this includes churches in the Holy Land. The use of mosaic, imported marble, and sculpted stone decoration in general supports that interpretation, as would the possible presence of a cemetery.

Working from this evidence, the nuns recognized that they had found a major Byzantine and medieval church. They also realized that, like the Large Cave, this building had been used in the medieval period and then destroyed by fire. Together, the evidence from the nuns' excavations told a consistent and compelling story.

Anyone would think that the nuns would have become celebrated by archaeologists for these discoveries. At the very least it might be supposed that Mère Giraud and her successor as superior would be hailed as great archaeologists. However, the convent met with a series of problems which unfairly affected their reputation at the time.

When Mère Giraud published an outline of what the nuns had found in an academic journal called the *Revue Illustrée de la Terre Sainte et de l'Orient Chrétien,* the reaction was far from enthusiastic. Whether it was because they were 'outsiders' to the Franciscan school of biblical archaeology, or because they were nuns, or because they had embarrassed the 'biblical archaeologists' of their time, almost at once they came under scholarly fire.

Criticisms of their work and interpretations began to be published. In the 1890s and 1900s, it seems that they had no academic supporters. By the time World War I broke out in 1914, despite their recent discovery of what was plainly a large Byzantine and medieval church in the centre of Nazareth, the nuns were either ignored or derided. Their interpretation of the site was treated as fantasy.

But even worse was to come. During World War I, the convent buildings were taken over by Turkish troops and the nuns evacuated. When the nuns returned, they found that the archaeological features already exposed had been treated with disrespect and their museum ransacked. Even those especially precious finds which had been given by the nuns to local families for safekeeping during the occupation were often never returned.

No archaeological work was undertaken at the convent from the end of World War I until 1930, although a new and improved shelter for the underground part of the site—the present Cellar—was built in 1929. Perhaps the events of the war had prompted the nuns to take even greater care of the ruins on their land.

Others took an interest in the site for nefarious reasons. Obviously, reports of gold coins and other valuable objects at the convent could prove attractive to those with less lofty motives than the nuns.

Late in 1930 two men arrived at the convent saying that they were visiting Belgian clerics interested in archaeology. One, Alphonse Duhot, claimed to be a Catholic priest; the other described himself as no less than an abbot, Abbé Benoit. They gained permission to dig inside the Crusader chapel next to the southernmost tomb in the Cellar.

All that is recorded of their excavation is that they dug down about 5 metres and found only natural limestone. Such a big hole was left from this excavation that it totally removed the medieval altar and had to be filled with soil brought in from elsewhere. Once it was backfilled, the nuns rebuilt a copy of the altar on the basis of memory and an old photograph.

What these men were looking for is unknown. Perhaps it was buried treasure, because as he left Nazareth to visit Rome, Duhot took with him about forty of the 'most beautiful' coins from the convent museum, including a very large coin or medallion.

The nuns were told that Duhot died shortly after arriving in Italy. But suspicions were aroused when the superior wrote to the Catholic Church authorities in Rome about the incident, presumably asking for the coins to be returned. Their reply was shocking: the Catholic Church had no record of Alphonse Duhot!

Other dubious characters were also interested in coins from the site. A large hoard of bronze Crusader coins had been found during the nuns' earlier excavations and kept safely in the convent museum. In 1931 a group of what were said to be Italian Catholic seminarians—men training to be priests—offered to clean them for the nuns.

To do so, these men said, they needed to take them to Rome, and would return the coins after they had cleaned them by their favoured method. This was frying the coins in olive oil, which is, to put it mildly, an unconventional treatment for ancient coins. Unsurprisingly, the nuns never saw the coins again.

Whether the culprits really were seminarians is unknown, but the similarity to the other theft is striking. Both involved coins being taken by men who may have been impersonating Catholic clergy and who said that they went to Rome after their trip to Nazareth. However, it is impossible to know whether these incidents were linked.

Plainly, by the start of the 1930s unscrupulous people were willing to trick the nuns and rob the convent of its archaeological heritage. In the following years the nuns' generosity and trusting nature led to many of the more portable objects being stolen or given away. Ironically, it seems to have been the objects thought by the nuns to be first-century, or of other Christian significance, that were especially favoured as gifts.

It was only in 1935 that the nuns began to dig again. The reasons for choosing the particular time and spot to restart their work are unclear. Perhaps it was, in part, to replenish their museum. Whatever the reasoning behind their choice, the nuns excavated a 2-by-4-metre area just to the north of the wall which they called M4. Here, they found brown soil containing a lot of human bone, but apparently nothing else.

The next year, 1936, Mère Hélène, the convent superior, published her *Histoire des découvertes faites chez les Dames de Nazareth à Nazareth* ('History of the discoveries made at the Ladies of Nazareth at Nazareth'), and prompted a scholarly reaction against the nuns which reverberated for the next eighty years. Even when I began work at the convent in 2006, there were traces of this reaction to be found in Nazareth and elsewhere.

The following year, 1937, an academic paper by a Franciscan priest severely criticized the nuns' understanding of what they had found. This paper, published in an obscure Franciscan scholarly journal, might have had no more effect than the many other criticisms which the nuns had attracted for decades. Unfortunately for them, the young priest was Bellarmino Bagatti, whose subsequently dominant role in the twentieth-century archaeological study of Nazareth we saw in Chapter 2.

Bagatti made a new plan of what he could see in the Cellar. This is highly inaccurate, but his accompanying plan and cross section of the best-preserved tomb are, surprisingly, much better drawn and more precise. It is hard to account for this discrepancy in the drawings by the same man in quick succession. Perhaps he could illuminate the tomb much better with whatever lighting he had than he could the whole of the area in the Cellar, which had no artificial lights until 1951. Perhaps he simply assigned more significance to the tomb than to the rest of the site.

Whatever the reason for this discrepancy between his two plans, Bagatti also completely ignored the portable objects, the walls exposed in construction or by excavations outside the area enclosed by the Cellar, and the records from previous excavations. Nevertheless, he believed that he had made a more accurate record of what was in the Cellar than any previous investigator. In his 1936 paper he used his records to formulate a new interpretation of the features in the Cellar. They were all, he said, either Roman-period burials or parts of Crusader-period building, which had nothing to do with religious life at all.

First backed by the Franciscan establishment, and then carried along by his subsequent fame, Bagatti's views swept away those of the nuns. Looking at it today, this was an archaeological tragedy. It is hard to see how he could have prevailed without his early support and later fame. But his opinions became the accepted interpretation, and archaeological work by the nuns ceased. Furthermore, their work was seen as the discredited fantasy of fanciful minds.

This could have been the end of twentieth-century study of the Sisters of Nazareth site. However, even inside the establishment of Catholic 'biblical archaeology' there were those who disagreed with Bagatti about the site. One man decided that he would show the real importance of the Sisters of Nazareth site by himself. That man was Henri Senès, and finding out the truth about the site became his life's work. This is the subject of the next chapter.

4

Exploring the Venerated House

Henri Senès and his lifetime quest

Henri Senès was born in 1897 in Marseille, on the Mediterranean coast of France. (See Figure 4.1.) After having trained and worked as an architect, he chose to enter the Jesuit Order in 1925. He was ordained in the Catholic priesthood in 1933.

The establishment of the Pontifical Biblical Institute at Jerusalem in 1927, with the French Jesuit Alexis Mallon as its director, had a profound effect on Senès' subsequent career. Although a linguist by training, Mallon had become interested in the possibilities of archaeology for research on the Bible, especially the Old Testament.

Mallon himself excavated at a famous prehistoric site, Teleilat el-Ghassul (often called just Ghassul), in the Holy Land between 1929 until his death in 1934. He co-directed the excavation with Robert Koeppel, a fellow Jesuit, and the French prehistorian René Neuville, with whom he also directed archaeological surveys in the area around the Dead Sea. After Mallon's death, Koeppel continued the Ghassul excavation in 1936 and 1938.

In 1935, Henri was sent by Augustin Bea, head of the Pontifical Biblical Institute as a whole (the main part of which was based in Rome), to assist with the Ghassul excavation. Presumably, his skill as a surveyor and draughtsman, combined with his general architectural training, had been considered qualification enough for this role.

Although he was originally due to be in Jerusalem for only three months, Senès spent the rest of his life based at the Institute there, except for one visit to Europe in 1950. A brief obituary by a fellow Jesuit, Leopold Sabourin, says that he was one of the Institute's most popular and best-known figures. A personal detail which Sabourin gives is that a highlight of Senès' visit to Europe in 1950 was to see television for the first time!

Figure 4.1. An anonymous photograph of Henri Senès in the Sisters of Nazareth convent archive. With permission of the Sisters of Nazareth convent; from *The Sisters of Nazareth convent. A Roman-period, Byzantine and Crusader site in central Nazareth*, 1st ed., by Ken Dark, copyright 2021 by Imprint; reproduced from that book by permission of Taylor & Francis Group.

Henri was plainly an important figure in the team when excavation resumed at Ghassul, presumably because of his skills in surveying and draughtsmanship. He continued to work there after World War II, when the site was directed by Robert North, another Jesuit working for the Pontifical Biblical Institute.

Senès' involvement with Ghassul in the 1950s seems to have been more problematical than his earlier work at the site. There was some conflict between him and the new director. It is hard to say what the source of this disagreement was, but it is important here to note that Senès was working at Ghassul during his involvement with the archaeology of Nazareth.

Nevertheless, it seems that Ghassul was Senès' main experience of archaeological excavation other than Nazareth. Nothing at Ghassul is of similar date to any of the material at the Sisters of Nazareth site. Consequently, his familiarity with the relevant pottery, glass, and other artefacts must have been somewhat limited. Furthermore, the intellectual context for all this fieldwork was the theologically driven agenda of the Pontifical Biblical Institute, even if he was outside the Bagatti–Testa hypothesis and its dominant 'Jewish-Christian' interpretation.

Senès began working at the Sisters of Nazareth convent after Mallon died. His interest may have been prompted by the contrast between Mère Hélène's 1936 *Histoire des découvertes faites chez les Dames de Nazareth à Nazareth* and Bellarmino Bagatti's rebuttal of this, published in the same year. Anyone visiting the convent with an open mind to its archaeology must have been sceptical about Bagatti's conclusions.

One might also suspect that so accomplished a surveyor and draughtsman as Senès would have realized that Bagatti's plan of the features displayed in the Sisters of Nazareth Cellar is highly inaccurate. Perhaps this was the, or at least a, reason that he became interested in replanning it in detail. Perhaps decades of subsequent work came from his understandable desire to get the plan right!

Senès plainly soon thought the nuns were onto something much more important than Bagatti had realized. It seems that his opinion almost from the outset was that the nuns had found both the house where Jesus had been brought up by Mary and Joseph (called by Senès the 'Venerated House') and St Joseph's tomb. In his unpublished notes he referred to the well-preserved rock-cut tomb in the south of the Cellar as the Tomb of St Joseph.

Consequently, in his work at the Sisters of Nazareth site Senès was undertaking a religious quest rather than simply trying to record the visible archaeological features. This quest became his life's work, with his final fieldwork at the convent not long before his death in 1963. So far as one can tell, he never wavered from his original interpretation, or considered any alternative hypothesis.

It would be a mistake to caricature Senès simply as an irrational fanatic in the pursuit of his goal. He was a serious and meticulous scholar, whose abilities as a draughtsman and surveyor are evident from the plans and elevations kept today in the convent archives.

His task, as he seems to have understood it, was to prove to the rest of the world that the nuns had discovered both the home of the Holy Family and the Tomb of St Joseph. He saw what he called 'architectural archaeology'—the study of ancient buildings—as the tool to achieve this. First, he needed reliable plans and elevations of what had been found at the site.

Drawing the ruins

Senès knew that all the existing drawings of the structures preserved in the convent Cellar were inaccurate. So, very reasonably, he set himself the task of recording more precisely what had already been found. Using his skills as a surveyor and draughtsman, he prepared detailed plans, elevations, and sections of all of the features which he could identify in the Cellar.

Drawing walls in the Cellar must have been a difficult job, because electric lighting was only installed there after 1951. Between 1936 and that date—the majority of the time Senès surveyed and drew the site—he must have been working from candles or lanterns. My own experience of being there shows how much would have been in deep shade or even utter darkness. It is to his credit that he made as few mistakes as he did.

Senès prepared a series of measured drawings and related them to a plan of the Cellar which he had made with a theodolite. Over all the years he worked at the site he was constantly revising and redrawing these plans in the light of new information, and producing more detailed close-ups of specific features which interested him. The doorways seem to have held a particular fascination for Senès—he drew them all in greater detail than other parts of the site at least once. It is unclear why.

Drawing the ruins in the Cellar in this way, he ran into three problems, which caused confusion to all later investigators of the site. The first problem is that he assumed that all the modern walls were completely vertical and had corners at exact right angles. These could, he thought, be used as fixed points from which to take measurements when recording earlier features. Consequently, the accuracy of his drawings came to rest largely on those assumptions.

Unfortunately, the walls stray from being strictly straight lines. This might be due to inaccuracies in their construction or to subsequent earthquakes, but probably a combination of both. Furthermore, the modern walls have corners that are not exact right angles. They are also less than perfectly vertical, probably due to the same combination of imprecise construction and earthquake movement.

Individually, these irregularities are minor. The Cellar and other buildings look well constructed. But they cause greater errors to accumulate over the distances measured, and cumulative errors crept into Senès' drawings unnoticed by him. This led to his plans and elevations being, to a greater or lesser extent, inaccurate.

Second, Senès tended to combine depicting what was actually there when he drew it with what he thought was originally there. That is, what he drew was sometimes as close to an accurate depiction of what he saw as was possible given his methods and equipment. But sometimes it was a reconstruction drawing, reflecting his interpretation rather than what he actually saw.

Unfortunately, in both the titles and captions of his drawings he omits to say which of these each drawing represents. This wasn't recorded in his notes, and so we have no way of knowing whether some drawings represent archaeological evidence which was simply more complete when he saw it than it is today, or are partial or complete reconstructions.

Senès confused matters further by labelling a few drawings as the 'present state' or 'reconstruction'. This leads to a false sense of security about what his unlabelled drawings represent. Some drawings without such labels are plainly reconstructions; others probably represent simple records of what was there.

Third, Senès was concerned mainly with walls—and doorways—and paid very little attention to showing other types of features, except cisterns. There is no indication that he was even aware of many types of archaeological evidence routinely found. Postholes, gullies, and even unpaved floors have no role in his descriptions.

Although Senès' drawings can't all be seen as an accurate representation of the contents of the Cellar, they are generally indicative of what was there in the 1930s–1950s. That is extremely useful given later restoration, and they were a vast improvement on Bagatti's plan of 1936. It is salutary that they are the most accurate twentieth-century record of the archaeological features displayed in the Cellar.

Senès was much better at pulling together past, often fragmentary, drawings and other records of features found on the surface, or at least above the level of the Cellar. This enabled him to draw an overall plan of the site extending beyond the confines of the Cellar and including what were, even in the 1930s, long-destroyed features. This plan was, again, constantly updated by Senès during his decades of study of the convent, to also include his excavations and chance discoveries there and in the surrounding streets.

Senès in the museum

By 1936, the convent museum was already packed with archaeological objects of many different sorts. There were coins and other metal artefacts, shards of glass and sherds of pottery, along with stone objects of various sizes from beads and individual mosaic cubes to the shafts of stone columns that once supported parts of buildings.

Senès went through these finds, putting the smaller objects in wooden crates, cardboard boxes, and reused food boxes or tin cans. Old tobacco tins were a Senès favourite.

Most of the surviving objects in the convent museum were in these containers when I first saw them in 2006. Although some still had his handwritten labels, many were unlabelled. Judging from surviving French labels in several different types of handwriting, it looks as if, when he sorted through the finds, some were already labelled.

Using his own knowledge of finds from elsewhere and probably, at least for some items, existing labels, he attempted to identify and date the objects. Occasionally, his labels also give the find-spot or other details of the object. But most just give a category of objects, such as pottery or glass.

It might be expected that all the objects in the convent museum come from the convent. This was my own initial assumption when I first saw the museum in 2005. It seems to be an assumption shared with many others who have visited the site. But it is certainly incorrect.

Senès' labels note that some objects which are still in the museum came from locations outside Nazareth. These, he tells us, come from places such as Kefar Kana, Acre, and 'Eilaboun' (Eilabun). There were once more such objects, for example a now-lost pottery lamp described in his notes as having been given to the convent museum from the excavation at Tabgha on the Sea of Galilee.

There is no indication that any of the larger pieces of worked stone came from elsewhere. Many were certainly found at the convent, because they are described in the nuns' nineteenth- and early twentieth-century notes. However, even a piece of mosaic floor is described by Senès as being from the 'ancient tombs' of 'Chef-Amar' (Shefa-'Amr)—a site where Byzantine rock-cut tombs were found in the nineteenth century and where there was another convent belonging to the Sisters of Nazareth.

There is no suggestion that any of this material was being passed off as from the convent excavations. Neither the nuns nor Senès felt that they needed to fabricate anything to prove that the site was what they said it was. On its labels, the outside origin of the material is made clear.

Nevertheless, given that most of the finds in the museum are unlabelled, just because an object is in the convent museum doesn't mean that object was found at the convent. This, combined with the fact that many of the cardboard and wooden boxes, and other objects displayed on the museum shelves, are unlabelled, means that the vast majority of objects in the museum are useless for interpreting the site.

What is more, what is left in the museum is likely to be an unrepresenta-tive sample of what was found. Most visitors to the convent since the exca-vations began had understood the objects which the nuns had found in religious terms. These were relics from the time of Jesus, or at least artefacts from Nazareth which might be kept as souvenirs of the Holy Land. As such, visitors had often asked the nuns for something to take home—a coin, a lamp, or whatever.

Because of this, and their own generosity, the nuns had been giving away objects to visitors since the early twentieth century. Of course, pious visitors especially wanted those things that looked as if they might be from the early first century or had Christian symbols on them. Consequently, lots of things were given away, but what was given away was far from a random selection of what had been found.

It was mentioned in Chapter 2 that objects had been given to local fam-ilies for safekeeping in World War I, and never returned. The same happened in World War II. What sounds like a significant quantity of the 'best' finds were taken to France for safety. What then happened to them is unknown. Perhaps they were destroyed by bombing, stolen, or lost. They may yet be found, perhaps in Marseille if Senès sent them home for safekeeping.

Anyway, by the time Senès came to describe the museum's contents much had already gone. It is apparent from his unpublished notes that he was well aware of this. Nevertheless, he did think that the coins in the museum were from the convent. This led to one of the most puzzling and enigmatic incidents in the archaeological study of the site.

A curious case of coins

After brief military service in the French air force based in Beirut, Senès was at the convent during World War II, when Nazareth was under British control. Indeed, the city was an important base for British troops.

Even in the early twenty-first century, the presence of British soldiers in Nazareth was remembered by local people. For example, walking down the main street in front of the Church of the Annunciation late in 2006, I came upon a hot-chestnut seller with a handcart very similar to those which I had often seen back in London at the same time of year. When I remarked on the similarity, the hot-chestnut seller said that this was a custom specific to Nazareth, which local people had got from the 'Tommies'—British soldiers—in the war.

This may seem unrelated to the coins in the convent museum, but remarkably it was one of the 'Tommies' who Senès asked to identify them. In 1941 he showed them to Sergeant Lathan, a British soldier stationed in Nazareth, who was visiting the convent. Lathan said that before being called up into the army he worked at the British Museum. Apparently, there he was an expert on coins.

Whether this was true is uncertain. Having asked the Museum, there seems to be no record of a Lathan (or Latham, a more common British surname) ever working for it. But the identifications Lathan offered do seem possible given earlier descriptions of the coins.

According to Senès, Lathan said that the coins included a fourth-century *minim* of the Roman emperor Maximian, a Roman coin of the fourth-century Constantinian dynasty, five Persian coins of the sixth century, three silver Arab coins dating to the seventh and eighth centuries, three tenth-century Byzantine coins, four twelfth-century Crusader coins, eighteen Arab coins of the fourteenth and early fifteenth centuries, and nearly 200 Islamic bronze coins dating between the seventh and tenth centuries.

It seems that Lathan knew the appropriate technical language to describe the coins. The time span and cultural associations which he suggested would also fit in with what is today understood of the history of early Nazareth. So, regardless of whether or not he was from the British Museum, maybe he knew something about coins.

What is even stranger about this episode is that, while the coin identifications sound credible, they are no match for the labels which were on the coins in the museum in 2006. Nor do they match the identifications of the coins themselves by a genuine British Museum coin expert (Sam Moorhead) for my own research project. That is, we have three lists of the coins in the convent museum: one by Lathan in 1941, one by Moorhead in 2008, and what was written on the labels in the convent museum, which I first saw in 2005.

The simplest explanation for this is that Lathan indeed correctly identified the coins he saw. However, these were later replaced in the museum coin-display cabinet by Senès—perhaps after a theft—with another group of now-lost coins from the convent, which he labelled. Finally, these coins were also stolen, given away, or lost, and replaced by those in the cabinet in 2005 and which Sam Moorhead identified in 2008.

The question then is, how many of these coins actually came from the site? Nineteenth-century records credibly describe Roman, Byzantine, and medieval coins being found, but whether they are the same coins identified by Lathan or Moorhead is uncertain. Nevertheless, all three coin lists share similarities in the date and type of coins, so it is possible that they may at least reflect the range of coins found at the site.

Combining these descriptions, the coins found in the Large Cave were probably Early Roman to medieval in date. The Early Roman coins only came from two of the graves. No Roman or Byzantine coins were found in the south part of the site today within the Cellar.

Senès digs

Senès also undertook excavations of his own at the convent. The first of these was in 1940, when he—or rather a workman—dug a 5-metre-deep trench intended to reach the bottom of a north–south wall on the north-east side of the convent garden.

This established that the wall was very well built. Senès thought it was a terrace wall. One of his notes in the convent archive says that there was a great depth of soil, about 7 metres, to its east, but only 3 metres to its west. If so, it would suggest that all the ground to the west of this wall had been terraced above the edge of the wadi (seasonal riverbed) to its east, although it is, of course, open to other interpretations.

More intriguing is a long rock ledge, about 3 metres high, said to run westwards on the south side of the wall. This could have been a natural irregularity in the rock surface, or it could have been a product of quarrying at some time in the past. It might even have been a rock-cut wall, similar to that found in the area covered by the south of the Cellar.

It is possible that buildings of similar date to the rock-cut walls of Structure 1 on the south of the Cellar had existed on the hilltop, in the area of the present convent garden where this ridge was located. We have already seen that the nuns had found evidence for Early Roman-period occupation on the hilltop, so this feature could be part of that.

Senès thought that the excavation had been inconsequential. But he was undeterred. Later the same year, he decided to have a new look at one of the ancient cisterns (C12) which the nuns had found in the nineteenth century. This was the cistern which could only be accessed by a tunnel, similar to the one mentioned in Chapter 3, which the nuns had built or reconstructed under the street south of the convent.

When Senès' workman hit the side of the cistern with his pickaxe, water poured out of the broken rock surface. The explanation seems to be that, far from being a rock-cut pit simply designed to contain water carried from elsewhere, it was actually constructed to hold the water produced by a natural spring at this very spot.

At this unexpected turn of events, Senès made a quick section drawing of the cistern and hastily retreated. He never returned to the cistern, nor realized that he had found a spring at the convent.

Senès dug again later in 1940. This time, his excavation was in the Chambre Obscure, where he thought that there ought to be an ancient doorway into the Large Cave to its north. (See Figure 4.2.) There was no doorway, but in order to find this out Senès had the convent servant dig up much of the floor of this room.

Senès proceeded slowly, layer by layer, but as he excavated the floor as a series of small squares it was difficult to interpret what was found. Rock collapse was a real risk. It might be today if any further excavation took place in the Cellar. Senès had to give up the excavation altogether in January 1941 when a crack appeared in the rock ceiling over the room. A disastrous rock-fall seemed imminent, and it was obviously unsafe to continue.

Undaunted, Senès remained determined to find new evidence about the site. Next, he turned his attention to the mortared stone wall covering the south end of the Large Cave. Here, he found that there was a layer of clay laid down by water—an alluvial deposit—as high as the wall itself, and its foundations had been cut through another similar deposit.

Figure 4.2. The Chambre Obscure, showing the blocked Byzantine niche in its west wall. Henri Senès' first excavation in the Cellar was in this room. The blocking in the niche is modern. Photo: Ken Dark.

There were, then, two of these alluvial deposits: one later than the wall against which it formed, but the other earlier than the foundations of the wall. These foundations were also above a layer of soil overlying the two graves (T1 and T2) which the nuns had found in the south of the Large Cave. The graves were, therefore, earlier than both the wall and the alluvial layer through which it cut.

Consequently, Senès' efforts to further understand the north of the Cellar had come to fruition. However, he had been expecting a doorway between the Chambre Obscure and the Large Cave, but none was found. He was expecting the cave to have been open on its south side before construction of the wall along its south end. Instead, he had shown that the Large Cave had solid rock across its south.

To try to understand what was going on, Senès returned to excavating in the Chambre Obscure. He was hunting for doorways again. This time he wanted to discover another doorway between the Chambre Obscure and the room to the south.

As in his previous excavation there, Senès dug in the room in small squares. These must have been at most 2 metres square for more than one to fit between the pavement in the south of the room and the rock-cut door of the Chambre Obscure.

Nevertheless, Senès was able to recognize that the doorway had begun as a rock-cut feature. This presumably resulted from excavation just inside the Chambre Obscure, as visible evidence at the site shows that he left the area immediately to the south of the doorway, and its stone base, unexcavated.

Inside the Chambre Obscure he also found a rock-cut ridge about 12 centimetres high, going straight across the room. Neither he nor subsequent commentators have been able to say exactly what the purpose of this ridge was. It might have been the base of an internal division in the Chambre Obscure as originally planned, perhaps for another doorway or internal partition, or a result of subsequent use. However, some interpretations can be ruled out. For example, it is so slight and low that it could never have been a bench or base of a burial *loculus*, like those described in Chapter 3.

This rock-cut phase in the Chambre Obscure was followed by one in which the doorway had been rebuilt with drystone walling, although only one course of this survived. While largely drystone, it seems that this wall was mortared to the natural rock below. The wall also incorporated a boulder, lying on the rock surface, and was mortared into the north, stone-built wall of the room.

Possibly at the same time as the drystone walling was constructed, a hollow in the rock at the bottom of the west side of the rock-cut doorway was filled in with rough stonework. The nature of this hollow is unknown; it could have been a natural dip in the rock, or a worn area associated with use of the doorway, or even a shallow pit in the interior of the room.

Within the Chambre Obscure, there were two successive layers of rubble. At least one—possibly both—of these layers was mixed with alluvial clay similar to that found in the Large Cave. The same waterborne deposit filled a crack in the rock on the north side of the room.

The later rubble deposit was on top of the boulder on which the drystone wall stood, but the same boulder overlay the earlier layer of rubble. As both rubble layers probably represent the collapse of the rock ceiling of the room during periods of disuse, they suggest one episode of collapse earlier than the drystone blocking and one after it. During at least one of these periods of disuse, alluvium had time to form as the rock ceiling gradually fell.

Senès also found an east–west void 90 centimetres deep, possibly for a timber partition or fitting such as a shelf, and an 80-by-8-centimetre cut in the rock wall on the south side of the doorway. This is also possibly for a timber fitting. However, the date of these features relative to the successive use and blocking seen in the doorway is unknown.

Quite how deep this excavation went is also uncertain. One section drawing shows a thick layer of soil below the floor of the Chambre Obscure, but this is labelled 'unexplored', and another drawing shows the soil in this area as being shallower.

There are a few finds in the convent museum which probably came from this excavation. However, the only object Senès mentions when describing his work in the Chambre Obscure is a pottery sherd, which he says was identified as being of the first or second century BC. Ironically, this sherd was found 'independently'—whatever that means (loose in previously excavated 'spoil' perhaps?)—by the convent superior, Mère Perinet, in 1940. However, the sherd is lost, or at least is unidentifiable in the convent museum, and so its actual date is uncertain.

Senès' next excavation gave him the opportunity to seek the evidence that he most wanted. It will be recalled that, to him, the whole point of digging at the site was to prove its biblical connection. Mère Perinet—the nun who had made the 'independent' find in the Chambre Obscure—decided to improve the floor inside the 'Venerated House'. As this was to happen, she gave Senès the chance to excavate there. He must have jumped at the opportunity. (See Figure 4.3.)

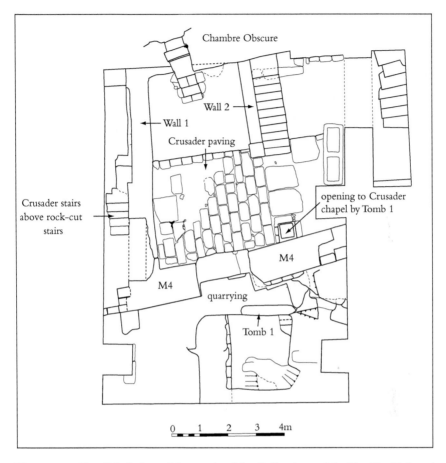

Figure 4.3. Simplified plan of the south of the Cellar (copyright Ken Dark), based on drawings on site by Ifan Edwards and Mitchell Pollington's plan for the Nazareth Archaeological Project. A detailed plan of the area within the Cellar is reproduced as Figure 0.4.

Fortunately, what was found is relatively well recorded. Indeed, Senès' notes and the convent diary provide eyewitness accounts contemporary with the excavation. Perhaps it was because he thought this part of the site was so important that he tried to record it in greater detail.

When Senès' workman started to dig, he first found a layer of soil and limestone fragments. This was above a layer of ash and charcoal mixed with soil, sloping up to the north. This must have made Senès recall the burning layer that the nuns had found in the Large Cave during their nineteenth-century excavations.

Many of the finds in the burning layer found by Senès were themselves burnt: burnt pottery, burnt stone, and what seems to have been a burnt limestone vessel. But there were also, possibly unburnt, stone and glass mosaic cubes—two sizes of cubes were present—and shards of glass vessels.

Given his perception of the material that he was excavating, unsurprisingly Senès carefully kept the objects from this layer together in a box. Perhaps this was just for later study, or perhaps he intended them to be taken away as religious relics. If so, he never got round to removing them.

The box was found in the convent in 2006, complete with its original contents and label. It even contained some of the soil in which the objects had been found.

Nevertheless, Senès' excavation methods remained crude, even by the standards of the 1930s and 1940s. (See Figure 4.4.) The workman simply removed the archaeological deposits with a pick and shovel, rather than each being recorded in turn and then at least the shallower layers being removed by trowel.

This method had archaeologically disastrous consequences. Although Senès believed that both the Virgin Mary and Jesus had walked on the floor of the building, he failed to recognize its actual floor layer. Consequently, his workman hacked straight through the floor, destroying most of it—what was left will be discussed in the next chapter. We know that Senès was unaware of this mistake, because his section drawings show that he speculated that the floor was at a much deeper level.

The disastrous dig of 1940 was by no means Senès' last at the site. During the next year, he investigated the area outside the convent walls for the first time. In December 1941 he noted a rock-cut cistern found in the street running up to the modern street market, where it passes the east side of the convent. A cistern is said to have been found in building work between the convent's east wall and this area in the early twenty-first century, but I have been unable to confirm this.

Later that month Senès got the opportunity to dig on the other side of the convent. The street was being widened and new sewers put in between the Sisters of Nazareth site and the Anglican church (Christ Church) to its west. This excavation showed that the east wall of the Anglican church was actually sitting on a much earlier mortared stone wall, presumably because this offered a firm foundation. East of this, on the west side of the convent site itself, he found other mortared stone walls forming small cell-like rooms, each with its own cistern.

Figure 4.4. Senès' excavation exposed in the restoration of the Cellar floor inside Structure 1 in 2010. The concrete plinth on its east to the left of the picture, the reset paving to the south and the concrete floor are visible. Large blocks adjacent to the scale may be traces of the, probably Crusader, wall which once divided Structure 1. The pattern of stones on the surface, although it looks like an interesting internal feature, is probably in twentieth-century backfill, and so nothing but a chance configuration. Photo: Ken Dark.

Later in the 1940s—the precise date is uncertain—he excavated at the southern end of the built wall, called by me Wall 2, running east of Structure 1. This excavation showed that the collapsed arch found by the nuns overlaid alluvial clay, presumably the same as that recorded elsewhere in the Cellar.

Senès also excavated on the other, west side of Wall 1, the main rock-cut wall of Structure 1, beneath the arched stairway cut into it. What he found is again uncertain, as the only record is an unpublished note. This seems to indicate some sort of crushed limestone floor.

The next thing that we know about Senès is that he was commended for 'exceptional courage' doing charity work with affected communities during the Arab–Israeli War of 1948–9. Senès also played an important administrative role in the daily running of the Jerusalem Institute.

While Senès was away, in 1946, Mère Perinet did an excavation of her own. She was interested in the area behind, that is to the west of, the main wall of the 'house', Wall 1, where Senès had dug in 1940. Unfortunately, she mistook the curving shape of the cut-back cave roof for the top of a curved tomb (an *arcosolium*), leading her to believe that she had found an Early Roman burial place. No finds in the convent museum may be ascribed to her work, nor is there anything to suggest that she found evidence of burial.

In 1951, a decision was made to reconcrete the floors in the Cellar and repoint the walls. This gave Senès the chance to dig again. He wanted to see if the massive mortared wall, M4, continued to the east. M4 apparently held a special fascination for Senès, for he returns to it again and again in his records, unpublished writings, and, finally in 1951, this excavation.

It turned out to be a deep excavation. Indeed, as it reached 4.5 metres deep, it must have been just to the east of the present east wall of the Cellar. This itself is odd, because it is hard to see how repointing the Cellar walls and concreting its floors would have occasioned an opportunity to excavate outside it.

Digging down 2.5 metres outside the wall, Senès reports that he found only dark soil containing pottery, bones, and pieces of glass. Under this deep layer he found further walls and what he described as a thin layer of sand. The latter was apparently another alluvial layer, within which he found the eastern continuation of M4 standing above the sloping surface of the rock.

Senès only dug at the convent one more time, in 1963. For his final season of work, he returned to that part of the site which he had first excavated some twenty-three years earlier. His target was a rock-cut cistern in the convent garden. There is no record of what was found in the excavation.

This final season of excavation was only a year before his death, of a heart attack, in a Jerusalem hospital on the night of 7 November 1964. He is buried in the small cemetery of the church of Notre Dame de France (today known as Notre Dame de Jerusalem), facing the Mount of Olives.

The Senès interpretation

Apart from two pamphlets, Senès never published the results of any of his archaeological work on the convent site. However, as already mentioned, numerous typescripts by him survive in the convent archives. In these, we see him work out an interpretation of what had been found. Some of them, and several of his drawings, look as if he was preparing a book-length report on the site, but that report was never completed.

However, another writer did publish some of Senès' work, even one of his plans, while he was alive and working on the site. How this came about is unknown. Did Senès approve this publication, or was he unaware of it?

This publication, in 1956, was by an author calling herself 'Soeur Marie de Nazareth' (Sister Mary of Nazareth). Soeur Marie's knowledge shows that she had access to the convent diary. She even knew legends about the convent unlikely to be broadcast outside its walls. She was, therefore, probably someone either associated with the convent or who stayed there sufficiently long to obtain this information.

At first, it might seem obvious that this necessitates that 'Soeur Marie de Nazareth' was one of the Sisters of Nazareth nuns themselves. However, although Soeur Marie was apparently a French-speaking nun, the Sisters of Nazareth keep the name given to them at birth, so she would be very unlikely to be called 'Marie de Nazareth'. When I asked at the convent, I was told that they knew nothing of Soeur Marie. Her identity, therefore, remains unknown.

This has long puzzled me. Having considered various options, there seem two possibilities which stand out as more likely than others. Perhaps 'Soeur Marie' might have been one of the nuns taking a deliberate pseudonym because she knew that publishing the article might be something disapproved of by others, either within her Order, in the Catholic Church, or in the scholarly world. Alternatively, perhaps she was a regular or long-term guest at the convent who was given access to the convent archive.

Senès' work was eventually described in a much more conventional way a decade later. A Canadian nun, Sister Renée Desmarais, wrote her 1966 PhD thesis on the site for the Department of Religious Sciences of the University of Ottawa. Sister Renée gives a careful summary of Senès's interpretation and reproduces his many drawings of the site. It is a reasonable description and overview of what Senès had achieved.

This begs the question of what, after more than a quarter of a century studying the site, was the 'Senès interpretation'? He thought that the earliest features were Jewish tombs, dating to the Late Hellenistic period. Because one of these—'the Tomb of St Joseph'—was on a lower vertical level than what he called the 'Venerated House', he thought that it was earlier than that structure.

Next in sequence, but after a period of disuse, came a series of cisterns—principally those today on the east of the Large Cave. Senès considered that at this time the site was a meeting place, comprising the south of what is today the Large Cave. He supposed that the meeting place was extended and a tomb set within it, which was then further extended to form the Large Cave. This was interpreted by him as a sort of catacomb, to use his term.

The Large Cave, he thought, was subsequently subject to unfinished modifications, before finally being elaborated with, among other alterations, a southern apse and possibly decorated with mosaic. Senès dated all of these modifications before AD 100.

Senès thought that, after a further period of disuse—estimated by him to be between 150 and 200 years—the cave was then further redesigned between 330 and 354. This was seen as associated with providing access to the 'Venerated House'. In his interpretation, the cave was further modified in a Christian context, becoming a crypt for a 'great church' of Byzantine date, also used in the Crusader period.

Senès, of course, paid great attention to reconstructing the 'Venerated House' in his unpublished typescripts and drawings. From these we learn that he interpreted it as a rectangular, partially two-storeyed, structure, with an eastern façade entered by two wide doorways with round-headed arches. He saw one of these doorways as springing from the built wall adjacent to the standing Crusader-style stairway, the other as an original version of the arch to the south of that wall.

Senès thought that all but one of the cisterns were unconnected with the house. He hypothesized that there had been a walled yard around the building, in which this cistern (designated C1) had stood as a chimney-like pinnacle separate from the block of rock containing the Large Cave located immediately to its west.

This produced an implausible structure, without close parallel when he wrote, or even today, but vaguely similar to modern traditional Middle Eastern houses. The pinnacle-like cistern in the yard is especially hard to parallel. There is little doubt that the structure which he called the 'Venerated House' had never resembled his reconstruction of it.

Senès was also sure who the occupants of the house had been: the Holy Family of Jesus, Mary, and Joseph. Consequently, in his opinion, Bagatti had been mistaken, and the nuns vindicated.

The response to Senès' interpretation

Senès' interpretation, although unpublished, has had a profound and endur-
ing influence on most subsequent discussion of the site among those
inclined to disagree with Bagatti's dismissal of it in the 1930s. By the 1960s,
there were effectively only two competing interpretations of the visible
features in the Cellar—those by Bagatti and Senès.

Like Bagatti and Senès, everyone else involved in the subsequent debate
from the 1940s to 1980s were clergy of one sort or another. That is, the site
became more a matter of religious controversy than archaeological discussion. Indeed, few archaeologists, even in Israel or in 'biblical archaeology,'
ever mentioned it.

So far as I am aware, the only person to propose a new programme of
archaeological study for the site after Senès, and before my own work, was
Dr Eugenia Nitowski (1949–2007), who at the time was a Carmelite nun.
Jeannie, as she was known when she wasn't a nun, initially studied healthcare
at Loma Linda University in America, before becoming a bush pilot in Africa.
She had been interested in archaeology since she was a child, and somehow
this led her to become the assistant curator of the Siegfried H. Horn
Archaeological Museum at Andrews University in America in the 1970s.

From the start of her time as assistant curator she was involved in the
excavation at Tell Hesban, co-directing the excavation of a tomb at that site
in 1971, when she would have been just 22 years old. Where, and how, she
learned field archaeology is unrecorded, but while she was at the museum
she gained a series of other qualifications: a master's degree in Religion from
Andrews itself, then another master's in History and a PhD in 'biblical
archaeology' from the University of Notre Dame.

Two other events during that time were to influence her later life. She
became a Catholic, and eventually a Carmelite nun. She also met Joseph
Kohlbeck, who had tried to sample ancient pollen from the Shroud of Turin
using adhesive tape.

Kohlbeck's technique of sampling surfaces for ancient pollen is problematical. As air almost always contains pollen, the pollen collected on the sticky
tape could date from any period in which the surface being sampled was
exposed, up to the time the sample was taken. But Jeannie was convinced
that the method worked, and tried to use it to reconstruct the environment

of an ancient tomb in Jerusalem to provide a comparison for pollen from the Shroud.

It was while a nun, based at Mount Carmel in Israel, that she tried to set up a research project to date the 'house' at the Sisters of Nazareth site. This was going to combine Kohlbeck's sticky-tape method of pollen sampling with dating pottery sherds stuck in the mortar on the built parts of the wall. The latter sounds as if it would be a good way to help date the wall, until it is realized that the mortar was replaced, and those pieces of pottery put in it, in the mid-twentieth century. The truth is that neither they, nor any pollen on the wall surfaces, offer a way to date anything at the site.

It is probably fortunate that Jeannie's Sisters of Nazareth project never began. Today, she is best known for her work on the medieval ruins at Mount Carmel. Eventually, she left the Carmelite Order and returned to America, where she founded a small biblical archaeology museum.

Others in the Catholic Church chose to defend Senès. The latest to do so was Jean-Bernard Livio, who wrote a brief popular article in a Catholic magazine in 1980, in which he argued that the Senès interpretation was correct. This was the article which I was given in the convent museum in 2005.

Unfortunately, Livio's article repeated Senès' mistake that the tomb was earlier than the 'house' and ignored almost all the portable objects found at the site. This phase of debate was effectively closed by Florentino Díez Fernández in 1995, who—responding to Livio's article—supported Bagatti's interpretation.

It is interesting that, although Senès, Bagatti, Livio, and Díez Fernández were all Catholic clergy, they disagreed in many ways about the interpretation of the site. Díez Fernández even doubted that any of the Byzantine stonework was originally from the convent site. He claimed that all of it had been brought in to build Crusader walls. This is extremely unlikely—detailed inspection of all the Crusader walls in the Cellar shows that there is literally no Byzantine stonework reused in them.

Nonetheless, the Sisters of Nazareth had become an almost forgotten archaeological site so far as mainstream archaeologists were concerned, worthy only of passing note for its well-preserved Roman-period tomb or its Crusader vaults and stairways. There it rested, until Sister Margherita took me into the Cellar in 2005.

5

Setting the record straight

By the turn of the twenty-first century the Sisters of Nazareth site had been largely forgotten by archaeologists. The few mentions of it were mostly in tourist guidebooks, and even these were brief and often dismissive. It was one such that had initially brought me to the site, as described in Chapter 1. When archaeologists did refer to the Sisters of Nazareth evidence, it was through the lens of Bagatti's interpretation.

So, in 2006 I was faced with a site that had never been closely examined, let alone published, by a mainstream professional archaeologist. The only people, it seemed, who were interested in it at all were biblical scholars. In the subsequent decade or so, even archaeologists who knew Galilee well would remark to me that they never knew it was there at all.

The first thing to do was to make a proper record of what existed at the site. Having got permission from the Sisters of Nazareth Order themselves and from the Israel Antiquities Authority—again, as described in Chapter 1— in December 2006 my archaeological team began work.

We started by sorting out the records of the nineteenth- and twentieth-century excavations and cataloguing the finds which remained in the convent. In the first instance, each object would need to be described and photographed.

Two considerations immediately came into play. First, although we had permission to survey the site in 2006 and access to the convent's records of previous archaeological work, there was no guarantee that this permission would be given again. Second, these finds and records were—it turned out—stored in many different places.

Some notes, drawings, and ephemeral publications, such as guidebooks for pilgrims, were in the museum itself. Others were stowed away in cupboards, and under or on top of them, elsewhere in the convent. One of the plans was framed and hanging on the wall. But most of the records were kept in the convent archives.

The convent archives were in a small modern room, recently decorated and well equipped, upstairs in one of the main ranges of the convent around the cloister. Importantly for us, it had a very good photocopier, capable of making excellent copies of the drawings, written records, and even such photographs as were left.

There were a lot of records to be copied. It took two people working full-time for a week to copy them all. When we were finished, nothing left in the convent from the previous excavations had been missed.

In 2006, another priority was recording the objects in the convent museum. For consistency we did this by filling in pro forma sheets for every individual object. These recorded the size, colour, material—such as pottery or glass—and a brief description of each artefact.

These forms were linked by a numbering system to colour photographs of every object. The photographs each contained a centimetre scale. In this way there was a double record—written and visual—of the size and appearance of every artefact in the museum.

In later years of the research project a selection of these objects was drawn to scale. This included all the artefacts which could be assigned a find-spot, but also all those which it was possible to date on the basis of comparison with those from other, well-dated excavated sites. These were to prove invaluable for dating the site.

Because there was no accurate plan, another priority was surveying the structures and other archaeological evidence contained in the Cellar. Consequently, a new plan of everything in the Cellar was made using a Total Station, an electronic surveying instrument capable of extremely precise horizontal and vertical measurement. This was undertaken for the project by a very experienced archaeological surveyor, Mitchell Pollington. (See Figure 5.1.)

In combination with the plan, elevations of the premodern walls in the Cellar, and sections of any surviving vertical faces of soil, were drawn by specialist archaeological draughtspeople, Ifan Edwards (our principal draughtsperson) and Helen Robertson, assisted by other team members. (See Figure 5.2.) Ifan and Helen made detailed stone-by-stone 1/10 and 1/20 scale drawings of the visible features and soil layers in the Cellar. Simultaneously, I photographed everything drawn, making a thorough visual record.

Figure 5.1. Mitchell Pollington surveying with a Total Station in the Cellar at the Sisters of Nazareth site. Photo: Ken Dark, with the permission of Mitchell Pollington.

In addition, I made a written record of every 'stratigraphical unit'—all the layers and features—visible in the Cellar. This was also achieved using pro forma sheets, similar to those used for recording objects in the museum. Using sheets of this sort instead of notebooks—as in nineteenth- and early twentieth-century archaeology—ensures consistency in written records.

Figure 5.2. Ifan Edwards drawing a section through Wall M4 during the 2006–10 survey of the Cellar. Photo: Ken Dark, with the permission of Ifan Edwards.

These sheets, based on the recording system conventionally used on archaeological excavations in Britain, asked a set series of questions, ensuring that everything was recorded consistently. As part of this system, the relationship of each layer or feature to those around it was recorded, especially which layer(s) or feature(s) it was underneath or overlay.

Using this detailed recording, it is possible to reconstruct the exact sequence of the archaeological features and layers in the Cellar. Relating these to the objects and to otherwise dateable characteristics such as distinctive architectural decoration or stoneworking techniques—notably the diagonal tooling typical of twelfth-century Crusader building blocks—these layers and features can be dated.

Often this dating is only to half-centuries, but it was sometimes possible to be more accurate than that. The significance of this is that, after more than a century of being exposed by excavation, the archaeological features visible in the Cellar can finally be assigned dates on a logical basis, acceptable to twenty-first-century archaeology.

This enables us to understand the sequence of structural events evidenced in the Cellar. It provides a firm basis for considering their interpretation in structural, social, and economic terms. However, in 2009 and 2010 refurbishment of the modern fittings of the Cellar offered two opportunities to go further in understanding the site.

In 2009, the 1950s wooden box sunken into the floor of the 'house'—that is, Structure 1—to hold a large fragment of the ceramic water pipe found in earlier excavations had become so decayed that it needed replacing. Removing the decayed twentieth-century wood, it was possible for us to record the sections exposed without further excavation. Removing the box also, of course, revealed what was under its base, which turned out to be the natural rock surface.

This enabled us to see, without excavating, that there was a considerable depth of soil inside Structure 1. It also showed that the wall on the east of the 'house' (Wall 2) stood directly on the natural rock surface. This opened up the possibility that Wall 2 was, in origin, earlier than the Crusader stonework in it.

This was deemed a success by the convent superior and, in 2010, we were offered the opportunity to remove the severely cracked twentieth-century concrete floor in Structure 1, ahead of the relaying of a new floor in this area. This gave us a chance to take away the concrete floor and the dump of modern rubble forming hardcore (the basis for a concrete floor) underneath it.

Carefully removing the cracked and broken concrete, and then the hardcore, we at first came upon what seemed to be a modern concrete shelf. This reached about halfway across the space between the main rock-cut wall (Wall 1) and the built wall incorporating two Crusader arches running along the east side of the house (Wall 2).

Where this shelf ended, there was a strip of what at first looked like dusty soil between the shelf and Wall 1. Once this was cleaned with a hand brush, it was obvious that it was another modern concrete floor. At first, we thought that this floor could be pressed back into service—saving the nuns the cost and bother of having a new one laid. But as it became cleaner, it was obvious that this floor was also so cracked and broken that it couldn't be used again. That was evidently why the nuns had replaced it.

However, the concrete step remained a puzzle. It looked twentieth-century. Then, searching through the convent archive for any clue as to its function, I found a photograph of the religious use of the Cellar in the mid-twentieth century. There was the concrete floor, looking new, and there was the step. It had been for a modern altar, the back of which leant against Wall 2.

The step seemed solid enough to reuse, but not so the floor. So, in conjunction with the superior, the decision was taken to remove this second broken modern concrete floor also.

When we did so, there was the predictable layer of hardcore. Again, it included obviously twentieth-century rubbish, like offcuts of rubber-coated electrical wire and a plastic name tag saying 'Canada'! But this layer was unmortared loose rubble. It would be better to base the new floor on something more solid.

We tried to remove the hardcore once again. This time it continued down—until we realized that this must be the backfill from Senès' excavation in the 'house'. Then, of course, we stopped digging.

Although this was a twentieth-century deposit, we knew what this layer was. Furthermore, there was almost no telling how deep it would be, except that Senès had managed to avoid breaking through the ceiling of the tomb below.

So that was how there came to be a large hole dug inside Structure 1. Journalists have mistaken it for an excavation by us. In fact, it was just an attempt at clearing away broken modern concrete floors and their hardstanding to lay a new concrete floor in the 'house'. All that was removed were demonstrably twentieth-century deposits.

But this process did expose a lot more of Wall 1 than was visible earlier in 2010. This had been unseen for decades, in fact since Senès' excavation. It also showed a surviving fragment of the east edge of the mouth of the natural cave from which Wall 1 had been formed.

What was especially exciting was that immediately next to the doorway to the Chambre Obscure there was a small portion of the original floor of Structure 1. (See Figure 5.3.) This was comprised of compacted crushed limestone with larger chunks of limestone included in it.

Embedded into the surface of this floor was a sherd of cooking pottery. (See Figures 5.4–5.5.) It was part of the same sort of Roman-period cooking vessel which we had found in the valley. At the southern end of the same cut—that is, of Senès' excavation—a small part of the natural rock was exposed, comprising chunks of stone surrounded by softer crumbled limestone. Senès' excavation had clearly gone deeper toward the doorway, but stopped just before it. Embedded into the crumbled limestone was another sherd of a cooking pot of the same sort.

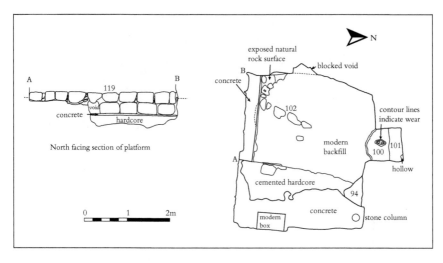

Figure 5.3. Plan of the area inside Structure 1, and section showing the north face of the paving. Drawn by Ifan Edwards for the Nazareth Archaeological Project; from *The Sisters of Nazareth convent. A Roman-period, Byzantine and Crusader site in central Nazareth*, 1st ed., by Ken Dark, copyright 2021 by Imprint; reproduced by permission of Taylor & Francis Group.

That is, the only two objects associated with these layers were both pieces of Roman-period cooking pot. Cooking pottery of this sort only came into production at the very beginning of the Roman period, so the floor—and most likely the structure which it was in—were probably Roman-period or later. (See Figure 5.6.)

It must be stressed that both the surfaces into which these pottery sherds were impressed were first exposed by Senès in 1940. In 2010, we only removed a deposit which had been heaped over them after his 1940 excavation. However, although he presumably saw them, he had failed to recognize the significance of the floor and sherds of pottery, although he had kept other objects from his excavation there—including a Roman-period spindle whorl and limestone vessel fragments. (See Figure 5.7.)

The excitement of finding what is probably the original, Roman-period floor of Structure 1 led the nuns to have a change of plan. The superior decided that they would carefully keep and display this piece of floor, and—filling up the rest of the cut to approximately that level—this is what they did. Today, the fragment of the original floor is on public view in the Cellar, behind a rope barrier.

Figure 5.4. The floor of Structure 1 seen from the south, with the doorway to the Chambre Obscure in the background. This and Figure 5.5 also show some loose stones, found to be in the modern backfill, omitted from Figure 5.3. Photo: Ken Dark.

Figure 5.5. The floor of Structure 1 seen from the north, through the doorway to the Chambre Obscure. Photo: Ken Dark.

Towards a new understanding

Archaeological recording at the convent, especially in the Cellar, between 2006 and 2010 led to a new understanding of the date and interpretation of the excavated features. This could be based for the first time on twenty-first-century archaeological concepts and logic.

Rock-solid evidence

Recording rock-cut features in much greater detail than before gave the opportunity for new insights into the stratigraphical sequence in the Cellar. While many rock-cut features were noted by previous investigators, the importance of the relationship between these went unrecognized. This was partly because they were unaware of the possibility of gaining stratigraphical information from such evidence.

Figure 5.6. Structure 1 looking from the south-east. Photo: Ken Dark.

Figure 5.7. Roman-period spindle whorl from Structure 1. For a reconstruction of how these objects were used, see Figure 6.5. From *The Sisters of Nazareth convent. A Roman-period, Byzantine and Crusader site in central Nazareth*, 1st ed., by Ken Dark, copyright 2021 by Imprint; reproduced by permission of Taylor & Francis Group.

Usually in archaeology stratigraphical sequence is recovered by observing superimposition—that is, by one layer overlying another—and features such as pits or postholes cutting through a layer. A different method may be used to extract that information from rock-cutting. This method is based on the same principles, but obviously cannot be based on superimposition in the same way as soil layers are superimposed.

A sequence is visible when one cut through the rock cuts away part of another rock-cut feature. A hypothetical example: if a bowl-shaped rock-cut pit A is cut into another identical pit B, removing part of the side of B, it is possible to say that A is later than B. On this site, if the rock-cut forecourt of a tomb removes part of a wall, which obviously once continued where it has been cut away, then the forecourt must be later than the wall. Elsewhere, such reasoning has been applied to reconstructing the sequence of construction of the famous rock-cut churches of Lalibela in Ethiopia.

Understanding the natural landscape is also important for interpreting archaeological evidence from the convent site. However, this had been overlooked by all previous investigators of the site. Senès knew the 'house' was cut into a hillside, but he never considered the shape of the hill except in reconstructing the building.

In Chapter 2 we saw that a seasonal river, a wadi, was the dominant natural feature within what is today the centre of Nazareth. It had also escaped the notice of all those who had studied the Sisters of Nazareth site previously that this wadi passed immediately east of the present convent.

The natural rock surfaces visible in the Cellar slope down to the south, so that the back garden of the convent is located at the top of what was, in the first century, a hill. This was the hilltop from which the cisterns adjacent to the Large Cave—containing the first-century BC or first century AD glass phials discussed in Chapter 3—were cut.

This hill fell sharply away just within the south of what is today the Cellar. In the south slope of the hill, in the southern part of the present Cellar, there was a small cave. (See Figure 5.8.) The mouth of this is visible today just to the east of Tomb 1.

The hill must also have sloped to the east because it had another cave in its east side. The roof of this cave is only preserved in parts of the main rock-cut wall (Wall 1) in the 'house'. The rock-cut wall had been formed by cutting back the cave, working east to west, giving an approximately flat terrace just east of Wall 1.

Figure 5.8. The Small Cave, a feature of unknown date and purpose.

This process of cutting back the cave made very clever use of the natural layout, or topography. It produced a head-high vertical wall of rock to the west, and east–west vertical faces of rock where the cut went into the hillside to the north and south. To create a wall to the south, all that was then needed was to cut back the southern face of the hillslope.

Once this had been achieved, the Chambre Obscure—in its original form—was constructed by cutting a doorway through the vertical face of rock to the north. There are then two possibilities. The open area of the Chambre Obscure, the actual room, might have already existed as another small natural cave. Cutting a doorway into it would give another room without much effort. Alternatively, the Chambre Obscure may have been dug out by working from the doorway and possibly also from its eastern end.

The remaining components of Wall 1—its back, or west side, and the strange rock overhang in its north-west corner—are also explained by this new analysis. The hill had been cut back behind Wall 1 to make it a free-standing rock wall. This wall was much stronger than the mortared rubble used for Galilean houses from the Roman period until the nineteenth century.

Wall 1 had a broad top on which there had probably been a drystone wall. When the rock was cut back by the builders, sufficient had been retained for a staircase to also be cut out of the rock. This gave access to the top of the free-standing rock-cut wall, on the level of the top of the overhang.

The top of the overhang had been deliberately smoothed flat so as to act as a support for something. Given that the stairs allowed one to climb up to this level, either an upper storey or flat timber roof may have been supported by the overhang. A timber roof or the timbers of an upper floor would, of course, have rotted away completely over the centuries, so that all that would be left were the rock components of this arrangement.

The twenty-first-century work also shed new light on the origins of the overhang. Once it is realized that Wall 1 was constructed out of a hillside with a natural cave, the overhang is recognizable as the last bit of the roof of the cave east of Wall 1. Another part of the cave roof was shaped and smoothed to form an arch beneath the rock-cut stairway.

The form of the original roof of the Chambre Obscure, before the medieval vaulting which covers it today, is uncertain. The rock-cut walls could, like those to its south, have been open and covered with a timber roof, or the natural rock may have been retained to form a ceiling.

When the concrete floors and their twentieth-century hardstanding in Structure 1 were removed, we also found that the last surviving fragment of the mouth of the natural cave still existed. This was immediately next to the west side of the doorway leading north into the Chambre Obscure.

Leaving enough of the overhang to support an upper-level floor, while cutting the cave away, took considerable knowledge of stoneworking and of the structural properties of the rock. This skill is also evident in the shaping of the roof of the cave to form an arch beneath the stairway. Whoever constructed Wall 1 and its rock-cut stairway was an unusually skilful stoneworker.

The opening in Wall 1 was blocked by a drystone wall when found by the nuns, and there were two successive walls built of stone on top of the rock-cut wall. These walls were, of course, first recognized by the nuns during their excavation. However, it is easy to understand why previous investigators of the site failed to recognize the other features. They were even unaware that there *was* a cave in this part of the site!

Consequently, our work led to a new understanding of the origin and function of the rock-cut features in what since the nineteenth century had been called the 'house'. It shows that these features really did indicate a structure (Structure 1). It also showed that Structure 1 was partly constructed by cutting away the limestone hillside to form a level platform and modifying a natural cave. Consequently, Structure 1 was built and used in the open air, rather than underground. Its present inclusion in the Cellar, therefore, creates a false impression of its original landscape context.

The local limestone is quite soft and could easily be worked even with simple iron tools, but durable enough to withstand the Galilean winter. Using these properties of the rock, a skilful stoneworker had formed a possibly two-storeyed structure out of the hillside with far less effort than it would take to construct the equivalent building out of mortared stone.

Obviously, the rock dug out in constructing these features could have been used for building further walls on top of the rock-cut ones. In fact, we found evidence of this—again unnoticed by previous investigators— immediately to the south of the area just described.

There, probably because the hillslope was of insufficient height to make fully rock-cut walls, a lower rock-cut wall was found. Fallen from this, and lying today where it fell, were the collapsed remains of a drystone wall. Such 'wall-tumble' is commonplace on archaeological sites. (See Figure 5.9.) Here, it probably indicates that a drystone wall stood on top of the adjacent rock-cut wall continuing the line of Wall 1 to the south. The rock-cut

Figure 5.9. The rock-cut wall, with adjacent 'wall-tumble', just south of Structure 1, and originally part of it. The scale is close to the boundary between the rock-cut wall and the 'wall-tumble'. Photo: Ken Dark.

wall had subsequently been cut away either by quarrying or tomb construction.

We had also discovered two more previously unknown stretches of rock-cut wall. One of these was poorly preserved underneath the mortared stone wall immediately to the east of the Chambre Obscure. So little remains of this wall that it could equally well have been a continuation of the wall of the Chambre Obscure or a separate construction to its east.

The other wall was north-west of Wall 1, in the base of the northern part of the twentieth-century Cellar wall. This rock-cut wall is similar in appearance to the others and continuous with Wall 1. It suggests, therefore, that there was another walled area immediately to the west of Wall 1, south-west of the Chambre Obscure.

How this western continuation of Wall 1 related to the hillside above it is uncertain due to the modern convent building. It could have been a free-standing wall such as Wall 1, or it could have been cut into the face of the cut-back hillside, perhaps for architectural embellishment or to take a drystone facing. Whichever of these options is preferred, this wall obviously continued to the west of the present Cellar.

These walls suggest that the rock-cut structure incorporating Wall 1 was larger than previously imagined. But this was by no means all that looking afresh at the evidence for rock-cutting, and the surface forms of the natural rock before it was cut, told us about the site. There was other, perhaps even more significant, evidence on the south side of the Cellar.

This comprised a series of rock-cut features in the area immediately south of the rock-cut walls just described. These at first seemed puzzling. They consist of a shallow shelf north of the abrupt natural hillside slope above the tomb with the rolling stone (which, following our site terminology, it is convenient to call 'Tomb 1'). Further up the hillslope to this feature are a series of more or less rectangular cuts in the vertical face of the natural limestone. One of these has an approximately rectangular boss of rock projecting to its south.

These features resemble rock-cutting found in the small Roman-period quarries just to the north of, and within, Nazareth. They are, then, best interpreted as quarrying. But here this quarrying had partly cut away the south end of Structure 1. Obviously, therefore, it has to be later than those walls.

These quarrying cuts were themselves partly cut away by a much larger, almost rectangular, cut—that of the forecourt of Tomb 1. This means that the rock-cut walls on the platform forming the level area at the top of the slope were earliest. Then they were cut by the quarrying, and then the tomb forecourt cut part of this quarrying away.

This sequence was confirmed by evidence immediately to the west. The low rock-cut wall continuing the line of Wall 1 was overlaid by the 'wall-tumble' described earlier. Above this there is a soil layer and, above that, an approximately flat mortar surface, probably a floor. Both the floor and the soil layer above it have obviously been cut away.

How this happened is uncertain, but the south of the rock-cut wall and part of the wall-tumble have been cut away by another larger, approximately rectangular, cut to their south. This cut strongly resembles the cut of the forecourt of Tomb 1. It is probably another forecourt for a rock-cut tomb just west, or beneath the west wall, of the present Cellar or a later extension of Tomb 1's forecourt.

Tomb 1 is distinctive enough to be approximately dated. As we saw in Chapter 2, rock-cut tombs can be divided into groups according to characteristics of their design. Those groups can be assigned broad dates by comparison with literally thousands of excavated tombs. On this basis, while rock-cut tombs were used over a very long period, from long before the Roman period until the Byzantine period, examples of Early Roman, Late Roman, and Byzantine date have distinctive characteristics. That is, if we can identify specific characteristics of the construction of a tomb, we can often assign it an approximate date.

Tomb 1 has several such characteristics. First, it is sealed by a large disc-shaped stone. Whereas small stone discs were used to seal Late Roman and Byzantine tombs, larger discs are limited to the period before the second century AD.

On this basis, Tomb 1 should date before about AD 100. It also has an internal round-headed niche, just by the entrance. These niches are typical of Early Roman-period Jewish tombs, which would be consistent with the date suggested by the large stone disc.

However, constructing rock-cut tombs such as Tomb 1 probably only began in Galilee in the mid-first century AD. Tomb 1 may, then, be at broadest dated to between the mid-first century AD and the end of the first century AD. Similar tombs of this date have been excavated just outside Nazareth at Migdal ha'Emek, but Tomb 1 is dissimilar in detail both from Byzantine tombs in the same cemetery and from later Roman and Byzantine tombs elsewhere in Galilee.

If Tomb 1 is late first-century AD, then the quarrying which its forecourt cuts must be no later than the first century AD. In turn, if that quarrying is later than Structure 1 to its north, which plainly continued south into this area, as the cut-away rock-cut wall indicates, Structure 1 must be no later than the end of the first century AD.

As we saw earlier in this chapter, the fragment of floor in Structure 1 contained a cooking pot sherd of a type manufactured only at the start of the first century AD. If the floor is associated with Structure 1 and cannot be earlier than the first century, and Tomb 1 cannot be later than about AD 100, the whole sequence of rock-cut walls, quarrying, and Tomb 1 must belong to the first century AD.

The same logic of stone-cutting also clarifies the sequence in the north of the Cellar. There, the burial places (*loculi*) in the south of the Large Cave are characteristic of the type found in rock-cut tombs. But if the south of the Large Cave was such a tomb, where is its north side?

There are traces of rock-cut features in its floor—the so-called 'bishop's grave', the grave with the ring mentioned in Chapter 3—and another very slight and enigmatic rock-cut feature to its east. Looking at these in the light of our new and more detailed records, it was easy to see what had happened. The Large Cave was constructed by cutting back the north side of an earlier rock-cut tomb.

When this happened, care was taken that the actual burials—which were in *loculi*—were undisturbed. This left the 'bishop's grave' on the floor of the Large Cave, and the *loculi* found by the nuns at the south of the cave, also mentioned in Chapter 3, in place. The enigmatic features on the floor of the cave elsewhere are just traces of its former rock-cut outline.

This earlier rock-cut tomb must, of course, have had an entrance. The only place that this entrance could possibly be—given that all other sides were uncut rock—was where the current entrance to the Large Cave is located. This makes sense also, as an entrance at this point would have been in the sloping east side of the hill.

Much more can be learnt about how the Large Cave was constructed. The cisterns on the east of the Large Cave are accessed from the cave by an approximately rectangular room and, for the southern cistern, a rock-cut doorway. The doorway shows that these cisterns had been used when the Large Cave was itself in use, as it would only have been possible to make it after the Large Cave was constructed.

However, as already discussed, the cistern nearest the entrance to the Large Cave contained glass vessels dateable to between the late first century BC and the first century AD. It was, therefore, in use earlier than the con- struction of the Large Cave. It seems likely that this was also true of the adjacent cistern to its north.

The presence of rock-cut cisterns in this part of the site may explain an otherwise puzzling characteristic of the Large Cave itself. As mentioned in Chapter 3, the ceiling of the cave near its curved north end contains a well- cut circular opening. This almost certainly functioned as a light well, letting sunlight into the otherwise dark cave, as it does today. But the opening and curved end of the cave also resembles the characteristic shape of Roman- period rock-cut cisterns in Nazareth.

It is possible, therefore, that the north end of the Large Cave was mod- elled out of a pre-existing cistern. Its light well would, then, be an enlarged version of the opening once used to get water out of the cistern.

Combining these observations, it is possible to suggest a sequence for the north part of the Cellar. First there were the cisterns, which were used for storing water associated with occupation on the hilltop in the late first century BC or early first century AD. Then, a Jewish rock-cut tomb was dug into the hillside below, with its entrance to the east. This tomb also contained glass phials of similar date, but it is unlikely to have been constructed when occupation was continuing nearby.

Both of these different uses of the hill probably date to the Early Roman period. Then, to judge from the coins found within it, in the fourth century, the Large Cave was constructed. It is probable that the positioning of the Large Cave was specifically in order to take advantage of the earlier cisterns and tomb. It is interesting to note that whoever built the Large Cave, which we have already seen was used—and probably constructed—as a Christian cave-church, respected and preserved the Jewish burials in the tomb.

There is, then, evidence of first-century activity in both the south and north of the site. It may be possible to identify two other first-century rock-cut features in the Cellar, although these are much less certain than the others.

Possible pits

The rock-cut chapel found by the nuns on the east side of Tomb 1 has a strange shape for a place of Christian worship. Its ceiling is domed, and its walls gently curved slightly inward. There is no religious reason why a chapel cannot have this form, but Bellarmino Bagatti wondered on the basis of its profile whether it may have reused a Roman-period rock-cut storage pit.

However, constructing this chamber had cut away the eastern *loculi* of Tomb 1, all except for their openings into the main chamber of the tomb. Consequently, if it is a Roman-period storage pit it must have been very shallow—and only enlarged to its present size when it was used as a chapel—or it would have to be later than the tomb. As occupation on a burial place was prohibited in Jewish law, the latter option is unlikely. If it was shallower, the resemblance of its profile to a typical Roman-period storage pit in Nazareth would be weakened.

It is, therefore, unlikely that the chapel east of Tomb 1 originated as a storage pit. It was probably constructed as a Christian chapel in the Byzantine or Crusader period. But there is another feature which might just be a storage pit of this type.

When Senès excavated the Chambre Obscure, he found a rock-cut pit in the floor of the room. While he had to give up excavating this feature for fear of rock collapse, his section drawing shows that it had a profile resembling those of Early Roman-period storage pits at the Church of the Annunciation. Indeed, the Chambre Obscure—a small windowless rock-cut room—seems perfect for storing foodstuffs or other perishable goods in a cool and dry environment, so it would make sense to have a storage pit there.

Possibly first-century walls

In addition to rock-cut features, there are also, of course, built walls preserved in the Cellar. Most of these certainly date from the Crusader period, as they show typical twelfth-century slanting chisel marks ('diagonal tooling') or distinctively medieval architectural characteristics. Diagonal tooling is found at many securely dated standing buildings, including in the Crusader version of the nearby Church of the Annunciation. But there are three places where earlier walls might possibly have been preserved.

During restoration of the box containing the ceramic water pipe, we found that Wall 2 was built directly on the natural rock surface. (See Figure 5.10.) However, some upper parts of Wall 2 certainly contain building

Figure 5.10. Wall 2, seen from the west. Photo: Ken Dark.

blocks finished with diagonal tooling. There is, therefore, no doubt that parts of Wall 2 belong to the twelfth century. But most of the stone used in Wall 2 shows no diagonal tooling nor any other distinctively medieval characteristics.

In fact, almost the whole of the north of Wall 2 is different in construction from its south. In the north of Wall 2 the only place where diagonal tooling occurs is on two large horizontal stones forming the upper part of the wall. These blocks continue the line of large stones forming the base of a window frame, which is itself identifiably medieval.

The line of large stones along its top, the window frame, and the whole south of the wall could, therefore, be later additions to an earlier version of Wall 2. Once these later additions are taken out of the picture, so to speak, there is nothing certainly medieval about this earlier form of the wall.

This cannot prove that the first version of Wall 2 has to be pre-medieval, just as it cannot be proved to be medieval. Obviously, if it rests directly on the natural rock, that offers no further dating evidence.

However, there are hints that the northern part of Wall 2 might be much earlier than the Crusader period. Unlike the south of the wall, it is made of irregularly coursed and roughly cut limestone, with larger stones at the bottom spaced by vertical stones. This style of construction is different from every recognizably medieval wall at the convent.

Nevertheless, the north of Wall 2 is similar to one of the walls in the excavated Roman-period house at the nearby IMC site. These similarities could be coincidental, but they could imply that the northern part of Wall 2 also dates from the Early Roman period. Interestingly, the medieval use of earlier walls is attested elsewhere in Galilee—including at the IMC site.

It is, therefore, impossible to say whether Wall 2 is wholly a twelfth-century construction, or if it originated as an Early Roman-period wall. If the latter, it was presumably the east wall of Structure 1. In favour of this interpretation, the southern rock-cut wall of the Chambre Obscure stops approximately where Wall 2 begins.

There may have also been built components to Wall 1. One of these may be mentioned by Senès in his unpublished notes. He observed that the inner part of Wall 2 was like the blocking wall of the natural cave as it passes under Wall 1. Unfortunately, it was Senès himself who dug away this blocking wall, and what is there today is a modern replacement.

If there was originally no blocking wall filling the opening through Wall 1, this would be very surprising. Everything else we know about the wall shows that it was very carefully made. In that context, it is frankly unbeliev-able that a gaping hole would have been left in its base.

It is, therefore, possible that Senès removed a pre-medieval, possibly even first-century, blocking wall from the cave opening at the bottom of Wall 1. But we know nothing about that wall, except that it was like the inner part of Wall 2.

Likewise, the earliest stone-built wall on top of the rock-cut part of Wall 1 could have been original to its construction. The present version of this is mostly built of uneven limestone but includes pieces of dark grey-black basalt, flint nodules, and a broken triangular fragment of a lime-stone slab.

There is nothing necessarily medieval, or even Byzantine, about this wall. But it has no characteristics suggesting that it is earlier in date. It could even be a modern replacement—like the blocking wall below it—for a wall dug away by the nuns before the 1930s.

Sadly, this leaves the wall-tumble south of Wall 1 as the best evidence for a wall built on any of the rock-cut walls. There were probably other stone-built walls in association with the original form of Wall 1, but the existing records of earlier excavation are insufficient to say anything about them.

Interpreting the Early Roman-period evidence

This analysis gives us several features which probably belong to the first century. The best-preserved of these—Structure 1—is the partly rock-cut room formed by Wall 1, perhaps also the original version of Wall 2, and the Chambre Obscure. Other rock-cut walls identified in the twenty-first-century survey may also be associated with it. Quarrying subsequently cut away part of the south of the structure, and that quarrying was followed by the use of the site for Jewish rock-cut tombs.

This later first-century evidence is easy to interpret, but the evidence for Structure 1 is so fragmentary—and so important to the overall interpret-ation of the site—that it requires further discussion. For the purpose of that discussion, it is useful to bring together what we know about this structure.

Structure 1 was constructed by first creating a level terrace and then cut-ting back the rocky hillside to its west to form free-standing rock-cut walls. These were high enough to support a roof above adult head height and solid enough to support an upper storey. They may also have had stone-built walls on top of them, but this is uncertain.

The stairway west of Wall 1 suggests that a roof covered the best-preserved room, and a roof may also be implied by the retained rock overhang within it. (See Figure 5.11.) The room probably also had a crushed limestone floor. The careful shaping of the retained cave roof beneath the stairway implies that care was taken with the construction of this structure, possibly even a concern for how it looked.

An extension to the south had been cut away by the later tombs, but was visible as the rock-cut base of a wall of which part of the drystone upper part was preserved by chance where it fell. The Chambre Obscure may have formed a subsidiary space, entered from the main room to its south by a partly rock-cut doorway. This room may have had a storage pit in its floor, and would have been well suited to storing perishable goods. Other stretches of rock-cut wall to the north-west and north-east could also be associated with the same structure, although this is uncertain.

Early Roman-period cooking pottery, limestone vessel fragments, and probably a spindle whorl and shards of vessel glass can be associated—to varying degrees of reliability—with this structure. Finds in the convent museum include plaster, which could also come from this early phase of Wall 1, again suggesting a concern for its appearance.

These finds and the care taken in construction support the interpretation that the structure was for human habitation. It is hard to account for this range of artefacts, or the insubstantial floor, if it was used for keeping animals. Likewise, neither an interpretation as an animal shed nor as a storage place for tools or produce would explain the apparent concern for its appearance.

Interpretation as nothing more than a chance configuration of quarrying is ruled out for the same reasons. Other interpretations, such as a place of burial or an agricultural facility, seem even less plausible. There is no reason to interpret it as a religious building.

What form this dwelling took is far less easy to ascertain. If the poorly preserved stretches of rock-cut wall are considered part of the same structure, this results in a plan virtually identical to that postulated by the expert advisors of the Nazareth Village reconstruction project for a first-century 'courtyard house'. This would be a family dwelling of several more-or-less rectangular rooms around a courtyard, with a stairway adjacent to one room leading from the courtyard onto a flat roof.

Figure 5.11. The Crusader stairway partially overlying the rock-cut stairway of Structure 1. From *The Sisters of Nazareth convent. A Roman-period, Byzantine and Crusader site in central Nazareth*, 1st ed., by Ken Dark, copyright 2021 by Imprint; reproduced by permission of Taylor & Francis Group.

Such houses are very well attested in the archaeology of the Roman-period Holy Land. They aren't usually mostly rock-cut, although they sometimes incorporate rock-cut walls. However, the hillside location of the Sisters of Nazareth might have led to the greater use of rock-cut walls at this specific site.

Alternatively, if the more poorly preserved stretches of rock-cut wall are left off the plan, it could resemble the sort of quarry workers' huts found in the Valley at Moshav Zippori, as described in Chapter 2. This would be a much more modest dwelling. Neither of the excavated examples of these huts in the Valley had an upper storey, but this could have been a more elaborate example, perhaps again because of its precise location.

It is very difficult to choose between these two possibilities. In my book on the Sisters of Nazareth site published in 2020 I considered the first more likely, with the proviso that the second was almost equally credible. In retrospect, I am even less certain that it is possible to choose between them on the basis of present evidence, although I remain convinced that they are the most credible way of interpreting the archaeological evidence.

Whichever of these interpretations is correct, there is evidence for a first-century domestic building—that is, a house—at the Sisters of Nazareth site. We can say something about its 'architecture', construction methods, and the associated, or probably associated, objects.

It is also possible to recognize that it was disused before burial took place on the site. When the tomb-builders arrived, the site was a quarry rather than a dwelling. But all this had happened within the first century, and that probably implies that we should assign the structure—however we reconstruct it—to earlier in that century rather than later.

Our work had, therefore, succeeded in recording the visible features in the Cellar to twenty-first-century standards and sorted out the surviving records and finds from earlier work. One consequence of this was to show that there was a first-century house at the site, and probably occupation of a similar date on the hilltop above it.

Our work also improved understanding of the Byzantine and Crusader use of the site. New information about Byzantine Nazareth was, of course, important for the overall research aims of my project. The Byzantine and Crusader periods at the Sisters of Nazareth site may also be of greater importance for interpreting the archaeology of first-century Nazareth than might be imagined.

Byzantine and Crusader evidence

The nuns had provided all the evidence to interpret the Large Cave as a cave-church, probably beginning in the fourth century AD. But the twenty-first-century survey added a lot of important new details. The first of these has major implications for how the Large Cave functioned as a Byzantine church.

No one had noticed a dark-green glass spout set in mortar in the side of the northernmost of the rock-cut basins in the north of the Large Cave. A narrow rock-cut channel leads down from the glass spout into the cistern in the north-west end of the cave.

As the cistern would have been inaccessible, the reason for this channel is likely to have been drainage. Initially, this might seem a strange thing to do. It makes more sense when you remember that there are circular holes near the base of each rock-cut basin, so that every basin would flow into another.

Given this arrangement, liquid piped into the southernmost basin would drain through the rest before coming out of the glass spout. Why anyone would want to do this may be explained by the geology of Nazareth.

Water seeping through the limestone would have contained a white chalky sediment. Putting it through a series of basins would allow the sediment to sink to the bottom of the basins. This process would provide especially pure water coming out of the glass spout and allow the collection of the chalky sediment, for whatever purpose, in the basins.

As we saw in Chapter 3, the nuns found a layer of ash in the Large Cave containing a complete pottery lamp. They also found two layers of alluvium in the cave. Some walls stood on the lower layer of water-deposited clay (alluvium); other features—including the steps and rock-cut channel—were below it.

Neither the nuns nor later observers realized that all the walls with diagonal tooling or Crusader architectural features are on this lower layer of alluvium. Nor did they realize that a vertical face of unexcavated soil is preserved in part of the side of the cave.

The sequence of deposits in the cave, as reconstructed from this section of unexcavated soil, is as follows. The original floor of the cave was overlaid after its use by limestone rubble 74 centimetres deep. This was in turn overlaid by stony soil 98 centimetres deep, and *that* was overlaid by a layer of soil containing a lot of charcoal, 58 centimetres deep.

Above this charcoal layer was alluvial clay about 1.1 metres deep—obviously the product of a prolonged period in which the cave was flooded with water. As the alluvial deposit reported by the nuns from the cave was described as about 1.6 metres deep, this alluvium is unlikely to be the same layer. The nuns' alluvial layer is also shown on Senès' drawings, which record its top as level with the top of the rock-cut basins. Neither the alluvium drawn by Senès nor that said by the nineteenth-century nuns to be about 1.6 metres deep could be the layer reported by the nuns as filling the Large Cave to about 40 centimetres from its ceiling (see Chapter 3).

This means that there were two separate episodes of flooding, each depositing alluvium. One was later than the Byzantine use of the Large Cave as a cave-church. All the recognizably Crusader walls in the Large Cave were built on this layer. The second layer of alluvium followed the charcoal layer which contained the late twelfth- or early thirteenth-century pottery lamp.

That is, the surviving section shows two things. First, that the nuns really did find a charcoal layer in the Large Cave. Second, it adds evidence that there were two episodes when the Large Cave was disused and flooded: one before, and one after, its Crusader use.

The Crusader restoration of the cave showed a lot of investment in the twelfth century. This is especially interesting because Nazareth was only taken by the Crusaders in 1099 and lost again in 1187. That is, these walls—some of which show two phases of construction—were built in the cave in less than eighty-eight years.

What is more, mortared stone walls in the cave must have been costly to build. Only aristocrats, rich merchants, and Church institutions could afford to build like this, whether they were in Europe or the Middle East.

This shows that whoever restored it in the twelfth century put a lot of effort—and probably money—into the Large Cave to make it look architecturally impressive. The stone-built basins on the surface of the first layer of alluvium were plainly meant to bring the long-disused, original series of rock-cut basins back into use.

This suggests that the Crusaders were restoring the Large Cave to be a cave-church again. Whoever did so knew something about how it had previously functioned and wanted to return the basins to their former use. That is, a memory of the Byzantine cave-church had probably persisted in Nazareth throughout the time that the site had been neglected.

The Crusaders also constructed a chapel next to Tomb 1, in the south of the area covered today by the Cellar. They built, or potentially rebuilt,

Wall 2 next to Structure 1 and added stairways to enable people to circulate through the underground area, which they reroofed with vaulting. They plainly thought that the tomb and the 'house' were important—maybe this, again, was based on a memory of the Byzantine understanding of the site.

Above all this was the large church found by the nuns. On the basis of twenty-first-century analysis of the convent archive and the remaining architectural stonework, we can reconstruct this church in general terms, even if its details are uncertain.

Byzantine stonework shows that the building was constructed in the late fifth or early sixth century, probably the former. It was decorated with imported white marble column capitals held aloft by granite columns. The walls and floors were decorated with mosaics. At least some parts of the wall mosaics were multicoloured and included gold-coated mosaic cubes, which would have glittered in the flickering light of candles or lamps.

The church probably had a gallery, judging from some of the architectural elements and the size of the columns, which also indicate a high structure. Because no roof tiles were found, the roof is likely to have been made wholly of timber.

The east of the church originally had three apses. Later in the Byzantine period, it was provided with a small side chapel on its south side. This was also decorated with mosaics and contained a stone sarcophagus, probably for a person of religious importance—perhaps a saint.

There was another building on the north of the church, known only from the nineteenth-century records of the nuns. It seems to have been a rectangular room 17 metres long with an eastern apse. It was supplied with water by a channel running underground from the area of the later 'Synagogue Church'. In view of its plan, size, relationship with the church, and association with water, it was probably a baptistery.

The church must have had a vaulted cellar (a crypt) adjoining the cave-church. This was accessed by a stairway with a monumental entrance of white marble, indicated by a frieze and other sculpture found adjacent to the cross-vaulted room. At the foot of the stairway there was a vestibule, or entrance room—the original version of the cross-vaulted room itself, which was also decorated with mosaics.

This vestibule led through a monumental rock-cut arch to the cave-church (the Large Cave), and along a passage—presumably lined with walls—to the area today in the south of the Cellar. In this area, both Structure 1 and Tomb 1 were decorated with mosaics, probably indicating that they were displayed and considered of religious significance.

This was, therefore, a large and impressive church with an equally impressive crypt, which included the cave-church. Archaeologically, a case can be made for the use of the church from the fifth century until at least the eighth, and maybe the ninth, century. After that it was disused and the crypt flooded, probably for at least a century given the absence of tenth- and eleventh-century finds, but rebuilt by the Crusaders.

The scale of the church presents us with a puzzle. On the basis of its preserved walls and apses, it may be estimated at over 28 metres wide and 35 metres, or more, long. The famous Church of the Annunciation—the building mentioned in most surviving Byzantine pilgrimage accounts—was probably just over half the size: about 15 metres wide and about 18 metres long.

The Church of the Annunciation was built on what the Byzantines thought to be one of the holiest places in the world: the site of the Annunciation (the announcement to the Virgin Mary by the angel Gabriel that she would give birth to Christ). If the adjacent Sisters of Nazareth church was bigger, and equally elaborately decorated with mosaics and marble fittings, why was it so large, and why was it located at this site?

The answer to the first of these questions may be that the Sisters of Nazareth church was the cathedral of Byzantine Nazareth. We have seen that from at least the late fifth century Nazareth was the seat of a bishop, and this bishop must have had his own church—his cathedral. The scale and decoration of the Sisters of Nazareth church would be appropriate for such a building. But, if so, why was it located here, rather than at the place of the Annunciation?

It seems impossible that a church such as this could have stood in the centre of Nazareth for hundreds of years without a single reference to it in any written source. So, we might start with those texts to see if they can explain why the Byzantine cathedral—if that is what it was—was built at this site, rather than at the place of the Annunciation.

Written descriptions of the Sisters of Nazareth site?

The earliest pilgrim account of Nazareth was written by the late fourth-century pilgrim Egeria. She describes a large cave in which it was said that the Virgin Mary had lived, and which had a well. By Egeria's time this cave had been converted into a cave-church.

Very few wells are known from Nazareth. Egeria says that Mary's Well, later the main well of Nazareth, was outside the settlement of Nazareth in her time. The well in the cave, which was inside Nazareth, has to be somewhere other than that.

The Sisters of Nazareth has the only spring known at a site with a cave in the area of ancient Nazareth. Unless there was a second, undiscovered spring at the convent, the water from this spring probably fed the cisterns and basins in the Large Cave. If this was true of the cave in the fourth century—and there are fourth-century coins from the Large Cave—then it might have given the appearance of a well in the cave. Even today, the opening once allowing water to be drawn from the cistern in the entranceway is commonly known as 'the well'.

On that basis, I think that Egeria was describing the Large Cave at the Sisters of Nazareth as it was in the 380s. Apart from the cave and the visible ruins of the first-century house (Structure 1) and tomb (Tomb 1), the appearance of the site at that time may have been of a rocky hill near a seasonal river valley (wadi).

The next description possibly relating to the Sisters of Nazareth site is in Adomnán's *De Locis Sanctis*, written in the late seventh century. This describes two large and impressive churches in the centre of Nazareth. One is the Church of the Annunciation, the location of which is—as we have seen earlier—well known. The other is described as near it, in what was then the centre of Nazareth.

Adomnán—abbot of the island monastery of Iona, off the west coast of Scotland—describes this second church as having a vaulted crypt, with a well from which water was drawn by a pulley. There were also two tombs in the crypt, and between the tombs there was a house said by Adomnán to be the house where Joseph and Mary brought up Jesus.

The Byzantine church at the Sisters of Nazareth has every one of the characteristics which Adomnán describes. It was a large, impressive church used in the seventh century—although built earlier—close to the Byzantine Church of the Annunciation. It had a vaulted crypt containing two tombs (Tombs 1 and 2), between which was a house (Structure 1).

There is even a cistern, which looks like a well, from which water may have been obtained by pulleys. Holes suitable for the attachment of such a device in the side of the top of the 'well' were identified when we recorded the elevation.

Consequently, the Sisters of Nazareth church is probably the second church in Nazareth described by Adomnán. If so, Structure 1 was considered by the Byzantines as the very building where Jesus Christ was brought up, and the family home of Joseph and the Virgin Mary. That possibility will be discussed further in the next chapter.

But first it is necessary to consider the third written account which may describe the Sisters of Nazareth site. This is by an Orthodox Christian pilgrim who visited Nazareth between 1106 and 1108. The pilgrim, usually known in English as 'Abbot Daniel', was an *igumen*, usually translated as 'abbot'. The exact location of his monastery is unknown, but it may have been at Chernihiv in the north of what is today Ukraine, an urban centre then experiencing a period of especial prosperity.

Daniel's description of Nazareth is both quite detailed and somewhat enigmatic. He says that he visited a three-apsed church in Nazareth. This had two stairways by which it was possible to enter a cave. A western door led into a small room on the right. Daniel said this room was connected with the upbringing of Christ. Daniel also believed that he had seen the house of Joseph in the cave.

At this point it would seem that he was describing the Crusader church at the Sisters of Nazareth. The above-ground church could be considered to have three apses, if the small chapel on its south was either out of use or if Daniel considered it irrelevant to his description. The Sisters of Nazareth Church indeed had twelfth-century stairways giving access to its crypt and, therefore, the Large Cave.

Other details mentioned by Daniel strengthen the impression that he is describing the Sisters of Nazareth site. For example, he says that the cave accessed by the stairways held the tomb of St Joseph. What Daniel describes as 'white water' was collected in the cave. Of course, this could be one of the tombs in the Large Cave, and the water could have been collected from the basins or other water features in it.

It might be surprising, then, to discover that twentieth-century scholars— and those of the first two decades of the twenty-first century—were unanimous in considering that Daniel's description refers to the Church of the Annunciation site. There are several reasons for this identification or, as I think, misidentification.

Daniel also saw a place within the cave considered by him to be the site of the Annunciation and tells us that there was a church dedicated to the

Annunciation above the cave. He says that the residence of the Crusader bishop of Nazareth was nearby.

This sounds like the Church of the Annunciation, which had been built on the site believed to be that of the Annunciation probably as early as the fourth century. The Crusaders rebuilt the church as their cathedral in Nazareth, and the Crusader bishop's palace was located next to the cathedral.

However, it is by no means that simple. The key to understanding Daniel's account is that he was an Orthodox Christian, rather than a Catholic. The Orthodox Church considered that there were two parts to the Annunciation, at two different places. Just to say that somewhere was the scene of the Annunciation leaves open the possibility that this was a different part of the Annunciation to that considered to be represented by the Cave of the Annunciation.

What is more, Nazareth was only captured by the Crusaders in 1099, less than nine years before Daniel was there. Given the time that it took to build late eleventh- and twelfth-century cathedrals in Western Europe, completing a cathedral in less than a decade would be very fast. It is hard to imagine that Nazareth's Crusader cathedral, a towering building 68 metres long and 30 metres wide, was up and running by the time of Daniel's visit.

Evidence that the Crusader cathedral of Nazareth was unfinished by the time of Daniel's visit between 1106 and 1108 is provided by an English pilgrim called Saewulf. Saewulf was at Nazareth at a date between 1102 and 1103 and records that the Church of the Annunciation had been badly damaged by the Muslims.

It is almost impossible that this damage happened after 1099, when Nazareth was securely in Crusader control. Saewulf's description must, therefore, refer to the old Byzantine cathedral—the one knocked down and replaced by the Crusaders, who literally built on top of it. The Byzantine building could have been damaged before 1099, and Saewulf could be reporting that.

If we interpret Saewulf's testimony in this way, it leaves only four or five years in which to construct the Crusader cathedral. Obviously, four or five years would be a ridiculously short amount of time to finish a 68-metre-long cathedral elaborately decorated with architectural sculpture. We know that it had such sculpture because of the fragments found when it was excavated. Furthermore, excavation also shows that the Crusader cathedral only had a single apse, whereas Daniel says that the church he visited had three.

Consequently, it is much more credible to associate Daniel's description with the Sisters of Nazareth site. If so, we have an eyewitness 'walk-though' account of the site in its early twelfth-century form. This is invaluable in telling us how at least one contemporary pilgrim, and probably medieval pilgrims more generally, understood what we can see today as archaeological features in the Cellar.

This has two fascinating implications for the archaeology of the Sisters of Nazareth site. First, it is one of the few instances in which an archaeological interpretation can be so closely compared with, and amplified by, a pilgrim's own experience of an archaeologically excavated medieval church. Second, it requires that the conspicuous twelfth-century architectural features in the Cellar which are apparently referred to by Daniel must have been put in place soon after the Crusader capture of Nazareth.

While hardly the same as building a massive cathedral from scratch, this comparison between Daniel's account and the archaeology of the Cellar shows how quickly many of the Crusader features there must have been constructed. These features created an impression of the church and crypt that was in keeping with the Crusaders' Western European Catholic outlook.

To give a few examples, the walls of the crypt (inside the Cellar as it is today) were clad with Crusader-style stonework and covered with Western-style vaults. The rebuilding of Wall 2 could have been intended to make it look like a Western European house, and the division of Structure 1 into two small rooms could express the medieval Catholic belief that Saints Mary and Joseph lived apart while married.

This diversion into medieval rebuilding may initially seem irrelevant to the identity of the Byzantine church, as interesting as it might be on its own terms. But the whole point of this building programme was evidently to restore the functions of the Byzantine complex, reworking these in an acceptable form to medieval Westerners.

That the church visited by Daniel was claimed to incorporate the 'house of the Nutrition' ('nutrition' in the sense of the upbringing of Christ) may be relevant to the possible dedication of the Byzantine church. If sufficient memory of the Byzantine use of the site remained locally to identify the function of the basins in the Large Cave, and to claim that Structure 1 and Tomb 1—decorated with mosaic in the Byzantine period—were theologically important, it is surely possible that the dedication of the church was remembered locally.

That is, memory of the Byzantine Church of the Nutrition probably persisted in late eleventh-century Nazareth, presumably among local Christians. This might be compared with the nineteenth-century story that there had been a 'large church' and the 'tomb of the Just Man' at the site— possibly the last glimmer of memory of the Crusader church on the site destroyed nearly 700 years earlier. Its ruins might have aided its recollection in the local Christian community.

All the written sources which can be connected with the Sisters of Nazareth site, therefore, agree that it was considered to have been the home of Mary. Two also claim it was the site of the house where Christ was brought up. On that basis, and especially given the testimony of *De Locis Sanctis*, it seems highly probable that the Byzantine church at the Sisters of Nazareth site was the lost Church of the Nutrition, the most important, previously unlocated, Byzantine church in the Holy Land.

Examining whether there could have been any factual basis to the tradition evidenced by these written sources from Egeria in the late fourth century to Daniel in the early twelfth century is best left until after discussing the question of what archaeology tells us about the rest of first-century Nazareth. This is the topic of the final chapter.

6

Archaeology and first-century Nazareth

Introduction

This chapter brings together the evidence considered in Chapters 1–5 to try to answer a series of questions about early first-century Nazareth as a place. Although these questions are unanswerable using written sources, archaeological evidence provides a surprising amount of information about the Nazareth in which Jesus was brought up and worked as a young man.

It is logical to begin with what the Gospels say about Jesus' Nazareth. The most extensive description of Nazareth in the Gospels—itself only a few paragraphs in a modern English translation—is in the Gospel of Luke.

Whether Luke had any direct knowledge of Nazareth has been much debated by biblical scholars. While accepting that Luke was writing about what he believed were actual events, some scholars have considered that his description of Nazareth was coloured by the Eastern Roman cultural context in which he wrote; others argue that he drew on limited, but genuine, information about Nazareth as an actual place.

There are, perhaps, three key points to consider in using Luke's description of Nazareth. The first of these relates to the language in which Luke's Gospel is written, Greek. Luke calls Nazareth a *polis*, which is often translated as 'town' or even 'city'. However, Luke's use of this term may be less precise.

While *polis* did literally mean town or city, the Gospels in general use it for a range of settlements, including those which were much smaller than a major Roman urban centre. It is telling that the term is used for the same settlements—places such as Capernaum on the shores of the Sea of Galilee—elsewhere described in the Gospels as 'villages' and called by the Greek term *kōmē*.

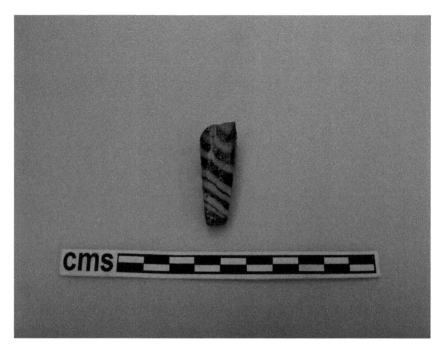

Figure 6.1. One of the earliest finds from the Sisters of Nazareth—a glass phial for perfume. From *Roman-period and Byzantine Nazareth and its hinterland*, 1st ed., by Ken Dark, copyright 2020 by Imprint; reproduced by permission of Taylor & Francis Group.

What we can infer from this is that neither *polis* nor *kōmē* was being used precisely by the Gospel writers. Twenty-first-century historians might want their sources to write in 'correct' Greek, but there is no reason to suppose that everyone in the first-century Roman provinces thought that terminological exactitude was essential.

Even more formal writers of the same period use *polis* very inconsistently. For example, the famous Jewish writer Josephus uses the term for both actual towns and smaller settlements. Ptolemy, in his *Geography*, uses *poleis* (the plural) for many settlements in Iron Age Ireland, although there were certainly no towns on that island at all during the Iron Age.

That is, we can dismiss the criticism that using the term *polis* makes Luke's description of Nazareth untrustworthy. But it does render it impossible to infer anything about the size, function, or culture of Nazareth from the term.

Equally unhelpful for our purpose is the description of Nazareth as on a hill. This is another point often thrown down as evidence of Luke's unreliability. However, as we have seen, archaeology attests first-century activity on the top of a hill and on a hillslope terrace at the Sisters of Nazareth site, and on a more-or-less flat location at the Church of the Annunciation and International Marian Center (IMC) sites.

Nazareth might be said to have been on a hill, or the slope of a hill, or on level ground. In fact, it was all of these. Again, this part of Luke's account of Nazareth can't be used to undermine his credibility, but conversely it is unhelpful in trying to reconstruct first-century Nazareth.

Finally, we come to the much-debated question of Luke's description of Jesus reading in the synagogue of Nazareth. Massive debates have raged among biblical scholars and archaeologists for generations about whether there were synagogue buildings in first-century Galilee.

Currently, a consensus seems to have been reached by archaeologists that there were purpose-built synagogues in first-century Galilee. Recent excavations have identified first-century synagogue buildings in both town and village contexts in Galilee. There are even two in the same Roman-period Jewish town at the site often called 'Magdala' on the west shore of the Sea of Galilee.

As an archaeologist, this would seem to me to settle the matter, but there is also another point to consider. Jodi Magness—an eminent American archaeologist working on Roman-period and Byzantine Galilee—has suggested to me that a synagogue could just mean an assembly for religious purposes, rather than an actual building. Considering that first-century Jews in Nazareth would have had to worship somewhere, then in one of these senses—a building or assembly—they would have had a synagogue.

This doesn't get us very far with understanding first-century Nazareth. There is no other reference in the Gospels to any building in Nazareth. In fact, apart from a steep slope down which people wanted to throw Jesus after He preached in the synagogue, they refer to no other specific place in Nazareth.

Nevertheless, the Gospels say that at least one craftsman—Joseph—lived in Nazareth. Although Joseph has often been said to be a carpenter, this is actually less than clear-cut. What Joseph is called in Greek is a *tekton*— which means a craftsman associated with building. This leaves open the possibility that he was a carpenter, but a *tekton* could also be a stoneworker involved in construction.

Consequently, the Gospel account simply describes Nazareth as having a synagogue—which wasn't necessarily an actual building—and at least one construction worker and his family. Given that someone had to build and repair the houses, this isn't a lot more than could be guessed by knowing just that Nazareth was a first-century Jewish settlement in Galilee.

What sort of place was first-century Nazareth?

It is often said that Nazareth was just a small village when Jesus was growing up. Historians and archaeologists have reached this interpretation for two reasons. First, as first-century Nazareth is rarely mentioned in written sources, it must have been very small and insignificant. Second, the approximate perimeter of the first-century settlement can be established by plotting the rock-cut Jewish tombs on a map. First-century Jews almost never lived on former cemeteries because of the rules of Jewish religious law.

In fact, both those grounds for establishing the limits of first-century Nazareth are erroneous. Nazareth was seldom mentioned at any time in the first millennium AD—even when it was plainly an important place, for example the seat of a Byzantine bishop, as discussed in Chapter 2.

Likewise, we can't use the distribution of Roman-period tombs to give us the outline of first-century Nazareth. All the Roman-period tombs in Nazareth are of types which could date from the mid-first century onwards. This has been used by so-called 'mythicists'—people who believe that both Jesus and Nazareth were fictitious—to claim that Jesus' Nazareth never existed at all. They are certainly wrong: there is, as we have seen in previous chapters, plenty of archaeological evidence for early first-century Nazareth. But it does mean that none of the tombs need date from the first three decades of the first century.

What is more, in first-century Jewish religious law there was no prohibition on constructing a tomb on a disused settlement. It was just living on, or in, a cemetery that was forbidden. So later tombs could be built on land that was once inside the occupied area of a settlement.

That is, neither of the two standard arguments that Nazareth was just a small village in the first century is sustainable. This is far from saying that Nazareth was a teeming metropolis at that time. In order to establish how big a place it was, it is better to look at the distribution of structures and finds associated with settlement—houses, storage spaces, and agricultural facilities—and then compare them to other contemporary settlements of early first-century date in Galilee. (See Figures 6.2 and 6.3.)

When we do this, an alternative picture emerges. The settlement evidence, outlined in Chapter 2 and at the Sisters of Nazareth site, suggests that a substantial area of what is today central Nazareth was occupied in the first century. This extends from the Sisters of Nazareth site to the eastern side of the present Church of the Annunciation compound, and from the White Mosque in the north to immediately south of the Church of the Annunciation.

Reconstructed in this way, first-century Nazareth looks like more than a hamlet. It encompassed an area equivalent to much of central Nazareth today. Even this could be underestimating its extent, because most of the area outside those limits has never been archaeologically excavated.

It is also instructive to compare what we know of first-century Nazareth's archaeology with the nearest first-century settlement, Yafi'a. Although often neglected in historical or archaeological discussions of Nazareth, Yafi'a is about 3 kilometres to the south-west of Nazareth—much closer than

Figure 6.2. A house, possibly similar in appearance to that at the Sisters of Nazareth site in the first century, reconstructed at Nazareth Village. Photo: Ken Dark, published with permission from Nazareth Village.

Figure 6.3. Detail of the reconstructed house shown in Figure 6.2, showing the use of a rock-cut wall in its construction. Photo: Ken Dark, published with permission from Nazareth Village.

Sepphoris. It has a strikingly similar set of archaeological attributes to those found in Nazareth, including similar storage pits, tombs, and portable objects such as pottery.

Unlike Nazareth, Yafi'a is attested by Josephus as a town which was a centre of Jewish resistance against the Roman army in the First Jewish Revolt. What exactly a town means in this context is—as we saw for Nazareth—hard to say, but plainly Yafi'a was more than a small village.

There have been many excavations in Yafi'a, and these have found a lot of evidence for the Early Roman-period settlement. This evidence includes a three-storey underground complex of ten storage pits, houses, quarrying, and tombs. The settlement at Yafi'a probably only began at the end of the second century BC or at the start of the first century AD. A series of hiding places date from the First Jewish Revolt itself, although no trace has been found of the double wall which Josephus says was built by its defenders.

From even this brief summary of the archaeological evidence from Yafi'a, the similarity with Nazareth is obvious. This leads us to a startling conclusion: there is no reason to doubt that first-century Nazareth is in archaeological terms a similar settlement to first-century Yafi'a.

Josephus never mentions Nazareth, but that is easily explained. The rebels weren't fighting the Romans at every single settlement in Galilee. They may have decided to make a stand at Yafi'a because it was located on a steep-sided hill and highly defensible, whereas nearby Nazareth wasn't.

If Nazareth and Yafi'a were the same sort of places in the first century, what type of settlement do they represent? There is nothing to indicate that either place was a major Roman town such as Sepphoris. But there is a form of settlement, common throughout the Roman Empire, of which both Yafi'a and Nazareth could be examples.

These settlements lacked public buildings, although they may have had a religious focus such as a temple, synagogue, or church. However, they provided a series of functions serving the needs of surrounding farms, such as craftworking or crop processing, and may have had traditional markets.

In the Western Roman provinces, archaeologists call this type of settlement either 'small towns' or *vici*. In what were the Eastern provinces, they call the same type of settlements 'large villages'. Whatever they are called, the settlement form is similar, and they were extremely common throughout the Roman world.

This interpretation would explain all the archaeological attributes of both Yafi'a and Nazareth. It would also explain the Roman-period pattern of settlements which my own survey of the valley detected. This suggested two patterns of small settlements, probably farms, one of which was focused on Sepphoris, the other on Nazareth.

This has been outlined in Chapter 2 of this book, but to recapitulate. All the objects used by people in the settlements near Nazareth—and in Nazareth itself—were produced by Jews. Those settlements close to Sepphoris had objects produced by Jews and non-Jews, reflecting the cosmopolitan nature of Roman-period urban society at Sepphoris.

This strongly suggests that those people who lived near, and in, Nazareth emphasized their own Jewish culture and identity. They seem to have actively resisted the market forces and cultural imperialism of the Roman province. In fact, Nazareth, Sepphoris, and Nahal Zippori may form the most clear-cut example of local people resisting Roman imperial culture anywhere in the Roman Empire.

This itself implies that Nazareth was more than just an insignificant hamlet. It was in some sense a focus for Jewish communities in the valley, in opposition to pro-Roman Sepphoris. This may be seen also in economic terms, with communities which avoided contact with Sepphoris and its culture using Nazareth as a centre for the local economy.

This raises another question. If first-century Nazareth was a centre for the local rural economy, what was that economy like? Archaeology can provide an answer for this also.

What was the economy of first-century Nazareth?

The construction of agricultural terraces, irrigation channels, and presses confirms that local people invested time, effort, and other resources in farming. Wine and olive presses attest the cultivation of grapes and olives, and the processing of these fruits into wine and olive oil. Building terraces, channels, and presses probably involved more than a single family due to the effort required, so they may also be evidence for separate families working together to increase production.

Farm animals were also kept for food and milk. The IMC site provides evidence of the rearing of cattle and sheep or goats—probably both. These animals could also provide hides for leather-making, and even their horns, hooves, and bones could be used to make objects.

There is, therefore, evidence of a farming regime which involved both growing crops and keeping livestock—that is, for what is often described as 'mixed agriculture'. This type of farming was usual throughout Galilee and in the Roman provinces as a whole. Here, the favourable climate and soils—outlined in Chapter 2—must have made it especially productive.

This raises the subsidiary, but crucial, question of how much of this produce farmers could keep. The many small settlements recorded by my survey and the IAA's rescue excavations and surveys imply the existence of a multitude of family farms. The similarity and limited range of the objects found on these settlement sites suggest that the people who lived at them were able to buy manufactured goods, perhaps at market in Nazareth.

This suggests that farmers could keep enough of what they produced to live on, and had sufficient left over to use to purchase goods which they didn't make themselves. The implication of this is that, whatever taxes they paid to the Roman authorities, they weren't the tenants of landowners taking most of their produce, and they weren't slaves. There is no evidence for Roman villas or a gradation of wealth in the settlements in the valley which would suggest wealthy landlords.

On this basis, we can envisage the area between Sepphoris and Nazareth comprising the farms of small landowners, rather than tenants of the wealthy. The picture is what would be expected of a Roman-period rural landscape without investment by the social elite. However, there is much more evidence for quarrying than might be anticipated in such a landscape.

Comparing the numbers of probably Roman-period quarries around Sepphoris with those around Nazareth, it is striking that there were twelve such quarries closer to the large Roman town of Sepphoris. This might be expected; after all, the stone for Sepphoris' many impressive buildings and shop-lined streets had to come from somewhere. But there are at least half as many—six or seven—quarries close to Nazareth.

Does this mean that we should imagine that Roman-period Nazareth was half the size of Sepphoris? If so, we would probably be looking at a large urban settlement, which seems unlikely given current evidence. More plausible is that the quarrying indicates a specialized role carried out by the population of Nazareth.

Rural communities in the Roman world often supplemented their income by various means. This includes settlements which have economies characterized by quarrying—appropriately enough called by modern archaeologists 'quarry settlements'. It is a serious possibility that Roman-period Nazareth was a quarry settlement in this sense, a primarily agricultural community which engaged in small-scale quarrying to supplement its income.

The advantage of this to small-scale farmers is obvious. If crops failed, or farmers had an unusually unproductive year, they could fall back on the income provided by quarrying.

The surviving evidence of these quarries shows that they were mostly used to extract approximately rectangular blocks and slabs. The most likely explanation for the blocks and slabs is that they were intended for the construction of buildings. The slabs might also have been used as paving for outdoor surfaces such as courtyards and roads. Stone vessels and weights were also produced in the Nazareth area, but this was probably only a minor activity compared to the cutting and shaping of these blocks and slabs.

This raises two intriguing questions. The first is where all these quarried blocks could have gone. Sepphoris had its own quarries, as we have seen, and there is a distinct gap between the part of the valley with quarries near Sepphoris and those close to Nazareth. So the building stone probably wasn't used there—especially if the people of Nazareth avoided contact with the town.

So, while some of these blocks and slabs probably were for use in Nazareth, the rest are likely to have been transported elsewhere. One possibility is Yafi'a, and/or smaller settlements in the Nazareth area. These could have provided sufficient customers for the small-scale quarries of Nazareth.

But getting the quarried stone to these customers would have been difficult. There is no evidence of a Roman road leading to Nazareth, and it has no waterway along which stone blocks could be transported. It is hard to imagine anywhere more landlocked than Nazareth!

The quarried blocks must, then, have been carried by wheeled carts—probably pulled by oxen rather than horses—along local tracks. The main alternative form of land transport, wooden sleds pulled by animals, is impractical on the uneven rocky terrain of the valley, unless using prepared tracks.

However, quarrying was by no means the only manufacturing activity going on in and around first-century Nazareth. There are hints at the IMC site that there may have been glass-working in first-century Nazareth. Glass-working more certainly took place at Sepphoris itself, at Moshav Zippori on the Sepphoris side of the valley, and probably at one of the sites identified in my survey of the valley (site 19). A series of circular features, probably ovens, also at Moshav Zippori, suggests another heat-based manufacturing process, although what this was is unknown.

It is probable that other objects found at the Church of the Annunciation, IMC, and Sisters of Nazareth sites were also produced in the settlement. For example, there is no reason to assume that the spindle whorl from Structure 1 at the Sisters of Nazareth or the loom weight from the IMC site were made anywhere else. Likewise, both provide evidence of textile production at those sites, although this was presumably just to fulfil household needs.

Nazareth was, then, probably a focus for a local economy including mixed farming, craftworking, and quarrying. It may have been used by surrounding communities as a marketplace and have provided them with products which they couldn't manufacture themselves. In this respect it was precisely the sort of place in which we might expect to find a *tekton*.

Living in first-century Nazareth

Archaeological evidence can also answer the question of what it was like to live in first-century Nazareth. (See Figure 6.4.) Underlying every aspect of daily life was that this was a Jewish agricultural community. Given the evidence from the valley and from Nazareth itself for the conscious rejection of Roman provincial culture, it is reasonable to assume that this community was strongly religious and anti-Roman in its politics.

In a first-century Galilean context, these attitudes required that life was governed by the requirements of Jewish religious law and the Jewish calendar. Before the First Jewish Revolt in AD 66 this would also have led to a perception of the world centred on Jerusalem and its famous temple. It is, therefore, credible that families from Nazareth travelled to Jerusalem for religious reasons at festival times, as Jesus is said to have done in the Gospels.

First-century pottery lamps found in and around Nazareth copy, and perhaps include, types from Judea (the area around Jerusalem), suggesting close contacts. Close connections to Judea might also be implied by the introduction of Judean agricultural practices into Galilee in the Late Hellenistic period identified by a leading Israeli expert on Galilean archaeology, Mordechai Aviam.

It is interesting in this respect that the rock-cut tombs found in and around Nazareth, and at Yafi'a and Migdal Ha'Emeq nearby, in the later first

Figure 6.4. Inside the reconstructed house shown in Figure 6.2. Photo: Ken Dark, published with permission from Nazareth Village.

century are also of Judean types. The Nazareth tombs show considerable wealth—both in the selection of the burial type and the objects found in them. Judging from the latter—glass vessels are the most frequent finds—these were high-status family burial places.

The presence of high-status people buried in Judean-style tombs from the late first century onward may be explained by the reference—discussed in Chapter 2—to one of the priestly families associated with the Temple in Jerusalem fleeing to Nazareth after the First Jewish Revolt. It is easy to see why they would choose devoutly Jewish Nazareth with its anti-Roman sentiments. The arrival of this family, and perhaps other Judean high-status refugees, might also have reinforced the already strident Judaism of Nazareth, and perhaps brought greater wealth to the settlement.

But this was all later in the first century than Jesus' Nazareth. Nevertheless, as we have seen, even in the early first century this was probably a population able to live well above subsistence level, if in no respect wealthy. Their houses—assuming that those at the IMC site and Structure 1 at the Sisters of Nazareth are representative examples—are likely to have provided comfortable shelter both from the cold and rain of the Galilean winter and the heat of summer. Their stone-built and rock-cut walls were probably smoothed internally with plaster, and they had floors of crushed limestone, almost giving the appearance of mortar.

These houses would have had flat roofs accessed by external stairs, as found at the Sisters of Nazareth site. These roofs, and courtyard areas outside the house buildings, could have been used as an extension of the living space of the house, as is well evidenced at many other sites. Roofs could also be used for sleeping in summer, when the inside of the house might get very hot.

It is possible that the summer heat was less a problem for the occupants of Structure 1 at the Sisters of Nazareth site, because of its thick rock walls. These would also have protected them very effectively against the cold and rain of winter, and required little maintenance.

The artificial underground spaces created for storing and processing agri-cultural products—as at the Church of the Annunciation site—could have been used for sheltering from the heat or rain while undertaking daily tasks such as food preparation, mending tools, or weaving.

Unless they were more decorated than current evidence suggests, the overwhelming impression of houses in Nazareth internally would have been the whiteness of the plaster and the limestone floors. Although it is uncertain to what extent they had windows in their walls—none are so far attested in first-century walls from Nazareth—this whiteness would have helped them seem brighter when illuminated by candles or oil lamps.

There is no evidence for what sort of furniture or soft furnishings (such as carpets and cushions) these houses had. But wood was relatively plentiful in Galilee compared to most areas of the Holy Land, and archaeological evidence attests household textile production in first-century Nazareth. It is, therefore, possible that they were furnished using these materials, perhaps in a similar way to more recent traditional homes in the same region.

The people who lived in these houses seem to have had a healthy and varied diet. They certainly had grain, grapes, and olives, olive oil and wine, but also probably other fruit and vegetables. Milk production, in addition to milk to drink and for cooking, probably provided them with cheese and yoghurt. They also ate beef, and probably lamb and goat. Wheat and barley were ground for bread, and possibly other baked foods.

As a community keeping to Jewish religious law, they would have stored, prepared, and eaten food in accordance with its rules. We have evidence of the red-coloured ceramic vessels used to prepare and serve these foods. Some cooking-pot sherds from Nazareth even have soot on their outside, showing that they were heated directly over a fire.

Storage pits and storage-jar sherds attest that sufficient was produced to save, and probably indicate planning for future needs. If every one of the known pits and cisterns were kept full, it would probably have been possible for this community to avoid the worst effects of crop failure or drought.

This all suggests that a fairly comfortable home life was possible. This may have been in contrast to the working lives of the same people. Farming, and the cycle of the farming year, must have been another dominant character-istic of life in first-century Nazareth.

Sowing, tending, harvesting, and processing crops must have been a near-continual activity. The very stony, if fertile, soils will have made ploughing with oxen especially difficult. When harvested, crops had to be processed and stored.

Animals had to be fed, protected from predators, moved between fields, milked, and eventually slaughtered. Terraces, olive and oil presses had to be built and repaired.

The wine and olive presses and storage pits at the Church of the Annunciation site show that some of these crops were brought into Nazareth itself to be processed. The size of the presses and storage pits also implies that here, at least, crop processing may have been communal work.

This last point might be significant for understanding who used these facilities. Carol Meyers—a prominent American specialist on the archae-ology of early Jewish communities—has argued on the basis of both written and archaeological evidence that women's work had a characteristically communal character in Roman-period, and earlier, Jewish culture.

From Meyers's analysis this would include tasks such as fetching water, cooking, and weaving. But here it could have involved crop processing using the olive and wine presses in and near the settlement at the Church of the Annunciation and Nazareth Village sites and elsewhere.

In addition to this, at least some of the community in and around Nazareth engaged in quarrying—cutting blocks and slabs and transporting them to where they were needed, as already discussed. The iron tools required to cut the stone were probably made in the settlement itself, which might imply at least one specialist metalworker.

This all enables much more about Jesus' Nazareth to be understood than would be possible from written sources alone. It certainly puts into context what it would have been like growing up there and living there as an adult. But can archaeology tell us anything specifically about Jesus or Mary, Joseph, and the rest of their family?

As an archaeologist and historian, my immediate response would be no. Unless, that is, the Sisters of Nazareth site really was where Joseph and Mary brought up Jesus. It turns out that whether this is possible is a more complicated question than might at first be supposed. Trying to answer it casts light on two other points of interest: the limits of archaeological and historical knowledge, and the length of time word-of-mouth recollection can be passed between generations.

Was the Sisters of Nazareth site really where Jesus grew up?

We can begin by asking the simple question—do we know that Jesus existed as a historical figure, rather than an invented person like James Bond or Superman? Like almost all professional archaeologists and historians who have worked on the first-century Holy Land—whatever their beliefs—I think that the answer is certainly 'yes'. But it comes down to the question of whether we have reliable written sources.

Self-styled sceptics about Jesus' existence—such as the mythicists already mentioned—often claim there is insufficient, or no, written evidence of Jesus as a historical figure. However, this is to misunderstand a few crucial facts about written evidence for people in the provinces of the Roman Empire, and specifically for first-century Galilee.

Hardly any of the millions of people in the Roman provinces in the first few centuries AD are mentioned in written sources. Those that are mentioned are almost always referred to in the context of wars or services undertaken for the Roman state, such as being in the Roman army or government. We have no reason to believe that Jesus fell into either category.

With the exception of Roman Egypt—where miscellaneous documents were preserved by a combination of specific practices of rubbish dumping and extremely dry conditions—most of the evidence for named individuals in the first-century Roman Empire comes from inscriptions. Outside major towns, non-military inscriptions, except graffiti, are usually only associated with burial.

Nazareth is very unlikely to have been a large Roman town, and it almost certainly wasn't anything to do with the Roman army. No first-century graffiti are known from anywhere near modern Nazareth, let alone in its centre. This leaves inscribed civilian tombstones.

Inscriptions of this sort are especially rare in Roman-period Galilee. In Chapter 2 we saw that none can be confidently attributed to Nazareth. This would hardly be surprising anywhere in the Roman Empire for a rural civilian settlement, but it is even less surprising in Galilee.

In fact, no inscribed tombstone commemorating a civilian craftsman is known from any first-century rural settlement in Galilee. Consequently, to say that Jesus or Joseph didn't exist because there is no inscribed tombstone commemorating them would be absurd.

At this point, it will be obvious that we wouldn't expect that there would be even one first-century written source for the existence of Jesus. However, unlike the vast majority of people who ever lived in the Roman Empire, there are several.

Written sources for the existence of Jesus

Jesus is, of course, mentioned in the four Gospels, the book of Acts, and the seven letters of St Paul, in the century after AD 30/33—the dates most often given by twenty-first-century historians for the Crucifixion. We usually think of all of these as parts of the Bible, but they were written as independent texts. Only later were they combined, with other texts, to make the New Testament.

There are, then, twelve separate written texts rather than one (the Bible) for the existence of Jesus as a historical figure. These texts were written by at least five—possibly six—different authors: seven letters by Paul, both the Gospel of Luke and Acts probably by the same person, and the three other Gospels written by separate authors. To someone used to working on other subjects in the study of the Roman world, this seems a lot of evidence for anyone in the first-century Roman provinces.

The twentieth-century Jewish historian Géza Vermes noted that most of the people mentioned in written sources for first-century Galilee are only referred to in a single text. Usually, this text was written by their supporters or enemies, rather than by some dispassionate unbiased observer.

If we were going to hypothesize from a blank canvas what written evidence we would expect if Jesus was a first-century historical figure, the evidence for this would consist of just one written reference authored either by a supporter or an opponent. But we have twelve, written by at least five authors, for the existence of Jesus. As the historical sources for most other named individuals from first-century Galilee were written by their supporters or enemies, we can't, then, dismiss these as sources for the existence of Jesus—no matter how we then analyse what they say in detail—on the grounds that they were written by Jesus' supporters.

There is also a point of historical method to consider. When it comes to assessing the credibility of these sources, it doesn't matter that billions of Christians today worship Jesus as God Incarnate—God who came to earth as a human being. The historical importance of someone shouldn't affect our willingness to accept their historical reality.

It doesn't matter that the stakes are higher in accepting the historical existence of Jesus than for a minor rebel against Rome whom no one except scholars has ever heard of today. There either is, or isn't, sufficient written evidence that a person existed.

By the standards used for 'uncontroversial' people in first-century Galilee—other rural construction workers included—if the Gospels were all there was to attest the historical existence of Jesus, they would be taken as more than enough evidence. Nevertheless, as well as the testimony of Jesus' supporters we have the evidence of writers outside of what we would call today the Church or Christian community.

In AD 93–4, only about sixty years after the Crucifixion, the pro-Roman Jewish writer Josephus wrote a book called *Antiquities of the Jews*. This might contain two references to Jesus, but one of these is so controversial—some scholars claim it was partially or wholly added later, others that it was in the original—that only the second reference provides really firm evidence. This refers to James, the brother of Jesus—today usually known as St James.

We may even add a further reference by yet another author. The famous Roman historian Tacitus refers in his book *Annals* (15.44) to 'Chrestus' (probably meaning Christ), when relating the allegation that the Christians started the fire in Rome in the reign of the emperor Nero. This passage is accepted as a genuine part of the *Annals* by most twenty-first-century historians.

That is, there are probably fourteen references to Jesus, written by at least seven authors, within about a century of the Crucifixion. These authors included both believers and non-believers.

This gives us much more evidence for the historical existence of Jesus than most of the characters filling the pages of textbooks on Roman-period

Galilee. Unless we want to reject most of the accepted historical narrative of Roman Galilee outright, we have, then, to accept that Jesus lived there in the early first century. The association of Jesus with Nazareth in Galilee is also evidenced in all four of the Gospels (Matthew 2:23; Mark 1:9, 1:24; Luke 4:16; John 1:46).

If Jesus existed and was from Nazareth, he almost certainly resided in the first-century settlement discussed in this book. Is it possible that the exact location of that house was remembered in later centuries? The answer depends on the relationship between our earliest written sources for Nazareth and memory.

Written sources and memory

The earliest recorded claim to know the exact site of a residence in Nazareth connected with Jesus is by Egeria in the 380s. As we have seen, she says that a cave-church was, or was at the location of, the house of the Virgin Mary. As it has already been shown that Egeria was probably referring to the Large Cave at the Sisters of Nazareth site, she was probably saying that this site was the location of Mary's house.

However, Egeria was writing about 350 years after Mary is said by the Gospels to have lived in Nazareth. This raises the question of whether an accurate memory of the location of a specific house could have been pre-served in Nazareth for three and a half centuries.

A similar question is raised by *De Locis Sanctis*, written in the late seventh century. This says that the crypt of a large church in central Nazareth con-tained the house in which Jesus was brought up by Mary and Joseph. Obviously, this could be a later version of the same story that Egeria men-tions. We have already seen that this was probably the Byzantine church on the Sisters of Nazareth site, and the house was probably Structure 1.

It is possible that a story about the cave-church in the 380s would be repeated by Christians in the 670s. Landmarks have been shown elsewhere by cultural anthropologists (scholars trying to understand the cultures of living communities worldwide) to be a sort of physical peg on which to hang stories or memories.

This could just be an example of that process, the Christian community in Nazareth being the context for the survival of this story, prompted by the continuing existence of the cave-church. In this way, the fourth-century associations of the cave could have been remembered as late as the seventh century. But if so, couldn't the ruins of Structure 1 have acted in the same way in earlier centuries?

Anthropological research on the relationship between house ruins and memory suggests that the ruins of people's homes often retain an association with specific families. Likewise, historical work on the relationship between house ruins, the demolition of houses, and the survival of memories also suggests that house ruins can facilitate, rather than erase, the memory of people or events long after the houses concerned are deserted.

That is, the ruins of Structure 1 could have helped preserve the memory of its former inhabitants. It is impossible to prove that this was actually what happened, but it *could* have happened. In a fourth-century village community of people whose ancestors had lived in the first-century village there may well have been stories—whether positive or negative, true or false—about its notable past inhabitants, handed down over generations.

This gives us a means by which there could have been a genuine association between the house and Jesus, preserved until the time of Egeria and then institutionalized by the creation of a church on the site. But it hardly necessitates that there was. It depends upon how we understand memory and the transmission of information by word of mouth over successive generations.

Anthropologists and historians have studied the process by which information is transmitted between generations by word of mouth in other situations around the world. Unfortunately, different studies have come to very different conclusions. On the one hand, scholars have long argued that memories are so easily manipulated and recast that they are an unreliable guide to the distant past. A commonly cited approximation to how long accurate memories can be transmitted verbally is two hundred years.

However, in recent decades anthropologists—including anthropologists working on their own non-Western cultures—have argued for the opposite. They have used events identified in archaeology or nature—such as volcanic eruptions or tsunamis in the Pacific—to assess the reliability of traditional stories of this sort. Several studies have found a close correlation between traditional story and scientifically demonstrable fact.

Consequently, there are grounds for a strong argument that a memory of the association of the site—and perhaps specifically Structure 1—with Jesus, Mary, or both might well have been retained over three and a half centuries to be recorded by Egeria. Conversely, by using another set of studies, we get the opposite conclusion: a strong argument that the association may have had no basis in historical fact whatsoever.

The modern history of the Sisters of Nazareth site may provide important evidence concerning the wider question of whether accurate information about places can be passed by word of mouth over centuries. In 1881, when the nuns bought the land for their future convent, they were told that the site was where a 'great church' had once stood and had the tomb of a saint, the 'Just Man'.

As we saw in the previous chapter, the Crusader church at the Sisters of Nazareth was a big building, with a venerated tomb in its crypt (Tomb 1), beside which a chapel was constructed. If Abbot Daniel's description does refer to the same church—and we saw in that chapter that it probably does—then this tomb was indeed believed to be that of St Joseph, called in the Gospels a 'just man'.

It seems that the memory of that church and the tomb, including the belief that it belonged to St Joseph, had been passed by word of mouth until 1881 in the Christian community of Nazareth. But the Crusader church probably burned to the ground in 1187. The site had subsequently been used for ordinary houses to judge from seventeenth- to nineteenth-century depictions of Nazareth.

There weren't even any ruins to prompt people's memories. The Crusader church wasn't visible after its destruction until the convent was being rebuilt in the early twentieth century. Then—as we have seen in Chapter 3—its ruins were discovered deep below the surface of the ground. If anyone knew of its existence in Nazareth in 1881, they must have got this information from word-of-mouth storytelling.

If accurate memories of the Crusader church were passed on by word of mouth from 1187 until 1881—a remarkable 694 years—we cannot exclude the possibility that a true story about the ruins of Structure 1 could have survived long enough to be told to Egeria 350 years later. Again, this doesn't mean that this actually happened, just that it could have happened.

It is, therefore, possible to construct strong logical arguments—backed up by historical and anthropological studies—both for and against the association of the Sisters of Nazareth site, even specifically Structure 1, with Jesus' upbringing in Nazareth. This might have been a genuine recollection of house ruins associated with the village's most famous inhabitant. But it could have been a made-up tale. We cannot say for sure.

Identifying pilgrimage sites

Two other points have also to be considered. Both concern how fourth-century Christians identified 'holy places'.

The Byzantine church at the Sisters of Nazareth is unusual in Galilee in being built on the site of a first-century house. Of the many Byzantine churches excavated in Galilee, there is only one other on the site of a first-century house. This is the so-called House of St Peter at Capernaum.

Capernaum, on the northern shore of the Sea of Galilee, was where the Gospels suggest that St Peter lived before, and for a time during, his recruitment by Jesus as one of the Apostles. The Byzantines constructed a polygonal church focused on one specific house in the first-century settlement at Capernaum, believing the earlier building was St Peter's house.

Polygonal churches were often used by the Byzantines to indicate an especially holy place. For example, there is one in Jerusalem at what they believed to be the site of the Ascension, when Jesus returned to Heaven. A Byzantine church built on the site of Mary's Well was probably of this form.

However, other church plans were also built to signify what were considered holy places. We see this at the Byzantine Church of the Annunciation in Nazareth, where a basilica—a rectangular hall with an apse at one end—was built at what was believed to be one of the holiest places in the world. That is, the polygonal form of church was far from being a universal characteristic of what the Byzantines considered especially holy sites.

What is important about the Capernaum church, in regard to the Sisters of Nazareth site, is that it was focused on a specific first-century house. By the Byzantine period, Capernaum must have been strewn with earlier house ruins of various dates. Why did the people who built the Byzantine church at Capernaum choose this specific, otherwise undistinguished, house?

At Capernaum, the answer is usually said to be that there was earlier Christian veneration of the same building. But a leading expert on the history of Christian pilgrimage in the Holy Land, Joan Taylor, has convincingly demonstrated that this veneration began in the fourth century rather than earlier. The question of why this specific house was selected remains, but concerns fourth-century Christians rather than Byzantines.

This sequence at Capernaum provides a close parallel for the Sisters of Nazareth site, albeit expressed in a different structural form. At the Sisters of

Nazareth we probably also have evidence of the fourth-century veneration of the site, the cave-church, followed by a more substantial Byzantine church.

Perhaps the fourth-century Christians who identified the Capernaum house had a tradition preserved by word of mouth from the first century. Or perhaps they just relied upon guesswork, or were guided by what they believed was a significant vision or other religious experience.

It is more surprising that at both Capernaum and Nazareth fourth-century Christians chose actual first-century houses to venerate in this way. They could so easily have selected buildings of another date or purpose, or features that just looked like earlier buildings. But coincidences happen— maybe these were just lucky guesses.

The probability of randomly selecting the ruins of a house specifically associated with Jesus in either Nazareth or Capernaum depends upon two considerations. The first is the size of the first-century settlements. The second is the ability of those who selected the building to identify houses from other building types among the whole range of ruins at the site.

To take a hypothetical example: if first-century Nazareth had twenty houses—a possibility for a community of, say, two hundred people—then the probability of correctly identifying a specific house would be 5 per cent. If the settlement had just ten houses, there would be a 10 per cent chance.

But this takes no account of the survival of features which looked like house ruins but weren't, or houses which didn't leave any trace visible in the fourth century. These might increase the likelihood of misidentification but also increase the chance of the ruins venerated being those of something other than a house.

Another line of argument comes from my recent analysis of cave-churches elsewhere in the Roman-period and Byzantine Holy Land. This has shown that caves under, or used as, churches were much rarer in the Holy Land than is usually supposed by archaeologists.

For her PhD, one of my former students, Eliya Ribak, compiled a catalogue of the 189 religious structures known at the time of her research from the Byzantine Holy Land. Eliya considered 139 of these structures to be churches, most of the others being synagogues. Just 18 (12.9 per cent) of the 139 structures interpreted as churches were cave-churches or churches built above earlier tombs or caves.

Most of these cave-churches were part of monasteries. Where this was so, the cave was associated with the veneration of a saint, often the founder of the monastery. None of the monastic cave-churches were wholly artificial caves, although some were natural caverns, reworked to make them more 'church-like'. A distinctive feature of these Byzantine monastic cave-churches was that the monks deliberately sought out natural caves, calling them 'churches built by God'. Other natural caves were used as monastic cells or retreats in the Byzantine period.

However, there is a small group of eight artificial caves associated with Late Roman and Byzantine pilgrimage sites. My recent analysis found an interesting and unexpected pattern concerning these artificial caves. Every one of them was associated in Roman-period written sources with episodes in the story of Christ in the Gospels. At some, this identification was clearly before the fourth century, when Christianity became increasingly accepted by the Roman state. It seems, therefore, that even before the fourth century Christians were locating events referred to in the Gospels at a few of the sites which later became Late Roman and Byzantine pilgrimage places. This evidence also suggests that they were constructing artificial caves to indicate those sites.

What is more, when first recorded in written sources, these caves each commemorated a different event in the Gospel story. This meant that they could be visited in turn as a sequence telling the whole Gospel story through its most important passages. It looks, then, as if we have here a pre-fourth-century Christian pilgrimage trail.

The Large Cave at the Sisters of Nazareth site is one of those eight artificial caves. Although no objects earlier than the fourth century were found within it, the cave-church could have been constructed earlier than the date of those objects. Nonetheless, the cave has to date from the Roman period, rather than earlier, as it is later than Tomb 2.

At the Sisters of Nazareth site, as we have seen, the earliest recorded association of the cave is with the house of Mary—later understood as being the place of the Nutrition, Christ's upbringing. Interestingly, the sequence indicated by the other seven caves has a 'gap' that this association would fit. If so, the association of the Sisters of Nazareth site with the house where Jesus was brought up may pre-date the fourth century, although there is no written record of it before the 380s.

Consequently, archaeologically and historically we can't say conclusively whether Structure 1 was the house where Jesus was brought up. This identification can be neither proved nor refuted. As such, it remains possible.

Even if Structure 1 wasn't precisely where Jesus was brought up, that location might nevertheless be on the Sisters of Nazareth site, perhaps where first-century occupation may be indicated under the nuns' garden. But it could have been elsewhere in Nazareth.

What can be securely established from archaeological and historical research is that Jesus existed and was associated with the place today called Nazareth. It is also certain that a settlement existed at that time in what is today central Nazareth, and so Jesus' childhood home was located in that settlement.

Furthermore, nothing known from archaeology or historical research contradicts what is said about Nazareth, or Jesus' time there, in the Gospels.

In this respect, it is interesting to ask what the archaeological evidence for first-century Nazareth might tell us about the place in the years from the return of Jesus as an infant from Egypt to Nazareth and the start of Jesus' mission, that the Gospels largely omit.

What if the Sisters of Nazareth house really was Jesus' childhood home?

The only written evidence for the household within which Jesus grew up is the Gospels. The Gospels of Mark and Matthew refer to the family of Mary and Joseph. They mention sons James, Joses (the same name as Joseph), Judas (who isn't the same Judas who later betrayed Jesus), Simon, and unnamed sisters. This might be considered a typical family in a first-century Galilean context, and they all—including Jesus—had names that were very common in first-century Jewish culture.

There is, again, nothing improbable about any of this. Nor, as we have already seen, is it implausible that Joseph was a *tekton* in Nazareth who passed on this trade to Jesus. If another group of texts written within a century said this about another family, historians would consider it unremarkable and probably accept it without the need to comment.

It is possible that such a family could have lived in the house at the Sisters of Nazareth site. Whether we adopt the interpretation that it was a partially rock-cut courtyard house, or that it was a quarryman's hut (for a discussion of this, see Chapter 5), there is sufficient room for nine or ten people to eat and sleep in Structure 1.

The objects found in Structure 1—cooking pottery, limestone vessel fragments, and a spindle whorl—would, as discussed in Chapter 5, be what might be expected from an ordinary house. They indicate neither greater wealth nor poverty than most Galilean dwellings of the same date. So the finds from the house might be taken to suggest a normal Jewish family life for this time and place. There is nothing unusual about them.

We might also expect a *tekton* to live on the outskirts of a settlement, where access to timber and/or stone was easier than in the core area of the settlement. If the Sisters of Nazareth site was on the periphery of first-century Nazareth, that might explain the later encroachment of first quarrying, and then burial, on its site when occupation ceased.

Much more interesting in this respect is that the construction of the Sisters of Nazareth structure, as we have also seen in Chapter 5, indicates considerable knowledge of the properties of the local geology. It also shows a high degree of skill in using and working with that stone. Structure 1 could well, then, have been built by a *tekton*.

As also discussed earlier in this book, archaeological evidence suggests that Jesus grew up in what was by contemporary, even local, standards a very conservative Jewish community. The people of Nazareth seem to have consciously separated themselves from their more cosmopolitan neighbours in Sepphoris. Their adherence to Jewish religious law is well attested by archaeology.

Consequently, preaching the inclusive message reported in the Gospels—a message of salvation for the Jews and all other people—might have been extremely unpopular with this community. This, in addition to the Gospel story about Jesus claiming to be the long-awaited Messiah when teaching at the synagogue in Nazareth, could easily have provoked the violent reaction which the Gospels recount.

Archaeology also suggests that the people of Nazareth might have had fairly recent links with the Jerusalem area. Consequently, it would be no surprise if people from Nazareth travelled to Jerusalem for religious reasons—as in the only detail of Jesus' childhood given in the Gospels. This also makes it possible that families from Nazareth retained connections with Judea, as the Nativity story of Joseph's association with Bethlehem (just outside Jerusalem) says.

There is, then, reason to suggest that the archaeology of Nazareth may support the credibility of the brief passages in the Gospels about Jesus' time in Nazareth and about Joseph's trade and Judean connections. Again, archaeology can't confirm that these events took place, but offers no reason to consider them implausible.

In contrast, archaeology refutes the modern belief that early first-century Nazareth didn't exist. This can, of course, be shown to be certainly incorrect by the evidence seen in Chapters 2 and 5. It also casts severe doubt on some twentieth-century suggestions about Jesus' links with Roman culture. It seems highly unlikely that the beliefs or attitudes of anyone living in first-century Nazareth would be influenced by Roman polytheistic religion or Greek philosophy, when the people of Nazareth wouldn't even use cooking pots and lamps made by anyone other than Jews.

For the same reason, the twentieth-century hypothesis—popular with some biblical scholars—that Jesus or Joseph went to Sepphoris to work is unlikely. It is more likely that people from Nazareth never even went to Sepphoris. Interestingly, Sepphoris is never mentioned in the Gospels.

The relatively isolated inland 'island' of conservative Judaism that was Nazareth may, then, have set the horizons of Jesus' childhood contact with the outside world. Other Jewish religious communities might have consti-tuted a network of acceptable contacts to the people of Nazareth—perhaps including social connections such as that involved in the story of the wed-ding feast at nearby Cana.

That is, archaeology can inform our understanding of the context of Jesus' childhood and early life as an adult. It may support the credibility of the Gospels' stories about Nazareth. It can also be used to refute the 'mythi-cist' hypothesis that early first-century Nazareth was a fictious place. But it neither adds to, nor contradicts, anything in the Gospels specifically about Jesus' time in Nazareth.

Conclusion

If Structure 1 at the Sisters of Nazareth site is the actual house where Jesus was brought up, it is a stunning discovery. It would enable us to identify material evidence directly associated with Jesus. But it is impossible to say for sure that it is.

Nevertheless, archaeology can tell us a lot more about first-century Nazareth as a place and everyday life there than can written sources. None of this material conflicts in any way with Christian beliefs about Jesus.

The following twenty points are among those established from the archaeological research discussed here:

1. An early first-century settlement existed on the same site as the present city of Nazareth.

2. This settlement was very probably identical to the Nazareth of the Gospels.

3. The settlement was in the centre of the modern city, encompassing both the Church of the Annunciation and the Sisters of Nazareth site.

4. The early first-century settlement originated in the Late Hellenistic period, and then was continuously occupied until the end of the Roman period and beyond.

5. It is possible on archaeological grounds that people in this community had migrated from the area around Jerusalem in the Late Hellenistic period and retained links with that area.

6. While the exact size of the first-century settlement cannot be ascertained using current evidence, it was more than a hamlet of a few houses.

7. First-century Nazareth's houses included well-built multiroomed structures, associated with objects indicating everyday life beyond a basic subsistence level.

8. The closest analogy for its archaeological evidence among neighbouring settlements is at Yafi'a, usually considered a small town.

9. Both men and women are evidenced within the settlement, and this—combined with structural evidence—indicates that it was comprised of family groups.

10. The settlement had a mixed agricultural economy, with people keeping animals for meat and milk and growing grain, olives, grapes, and other crops in the area currently under the modern city and probably in the valley between it and Sepphoris.

11. Crops were processed and stored in the settlement on a scale which suggests that it served as a local centre, that is a 'small town'/village acting as a central place in the landscape.

12. This was an exclusively Jewish community, religious and probably with an especial concern for ritual purity.

13. There was probably little or no contact between first-century Nazareth and Sepphoris, despite their proximity, due to the deliberate choice on the part of the people at Nazareth to keep themselves separate from Sepphoris.

14. Craftworking took place in the settlement of Nazareth.

15. The community was also involved in quarrying stone for building, per-haps more so than other neighbouring settlements.

16. Although the settlement probably wasn't involved directly in the First Jewish Revolt, its inhabitants constructed hiding places, suggesting that they were affected by the events of AD 66–70 or at least anticipated that they would be.

17. Rock-cut tombs indicate an influx of wealthy and high-status people in the mid- to late first century. The tombs show similarities to those in the Jerusalem area. None can certainly be dated to before about the middle of the first century AD.

18. From the Late Roman period onward, and possibly before, Christian pilgrims came to this settlement believing that it was the Nazareth mentioned in the Gospels.

19. A pilgrimage centre was established from the fourth century onward, focusing on places—including the Church of the Annunciation and Sisters of Nazareth sites—associated with specific events or people mentioned in the Gospels.

20. The Cave of the Annunciation and Sisters of Nazareth site, both foci of fourth-century and later churches, were in use in the early first century AD.

This is far from saying that written sources are of little value in under-standing Jesus' Nazareth, of course. They attest and date the historical exist-ence of Jesus, the association between Jesus and Nazareth, the involvement of Joseph and his family in building-related craftworking, the presence of literacy and a synagogue—of whatever form—in the settlement, and enable us to locate and put a name to Nazareth. For the later first century, textual sources also locate one of the priestly families from Jerusalem in Nazareth. All that would be impossible from any existing archaeological evidence.

The extent to which written sources for the history of Roman-period Nazareth correlate with the archaeological evidence is striking. These sources are telling us complementary—rather than contradictory—things about the same first-century community.

That is, whether one accepts the identification of Structure 1 at the Sisters of Nazareth site as 'the house of Jesus' or considers it just a domestic

Figure 6.5. A reconstruction of a first-century woman spinning wool, from Nazareth Village. Photo: Ken Dark, published with permission from Nazareth Village.

structure from the same settlement, archaeological research has made a significant contribution to understanding the Gospels' account of Nazareth as a place. There is, in fact, an archaeology of Jesus' Nazareth.

References

PUBLICATIONS ON WHICH THIS BOOK IS LARGELY BASED

Dark, K., 2020. 'Returning to the Caves of Mystery: Texts, archaeology and the origins of Christian topography and pilgrimage in the Holy Land', *Strata* 38, 103–24.

Dark, K., 2020. *Roman-period and Byzantine Nazareth and its Hinterland*, Routledge, London.

Dark, K., 2021. *The Sisters of Nazareth Convent. A Roman-Period, Byzantine and Crusader Site in Central Nazareth*, Routledge, London.

ESPECIALLY RELEVANT WORKS PUBLISHED SINCE 2020

Adler, Y., 2020. 'Ritual purity in daily life after 70 CE: The chalk vessel assemblage from Shuʿafat as a test case', *Journal for the Study of Judaism* 52(1), 39–62.

Adler, Y., Ayalon, A., Bar-Matthews, M., Flesher, R., Yasur, G., and Zilberman, T., 2021. 'Geochemical analyses of Jewish chalk vessel remains from Roman-era production and settlement sites in the southern Levant', *Archaeometry* 63(2), 266–83.

Fiensy, D. A., 2021. *The Archaeology of Daily Life: Ordinary Persons in Late Second Temple Israel*, Wipf & Stock Publishers, Eugene, OR.

Harper, K., McCormick, M., Hamilton, M., Peiffert, C., Michels, R., and Engel, M., 2020. 'Establishing the provenance of the Nazareth Inscription: Using stable isotopes to resolve a historic controversy and trace ancient marble production', *Journal of Archaeological Science: Reports* 30, DOI: 10.1016/j.jasrep.2020.102228.

Sherman, M., Weiss, Z., Zilberman, T., and Yasur, G., 2020. 'Chalkstone vessels from Sepphoris: Galilean production in Roman times', *Bulletin of the American Schools of Oriental Research* 383(1), 79–95.

REPORTS OF ESPECIALLY RELEVANT ISRAEL ANTIQUITIES AUTHORITY FIELDWORK AFTER 2020

Avshalom-Gorni, D., Najar, A., Tzin, B., and Yaroshevich, A., 2021. 'Migdal Ha-'Emeq' *Hadashot Arkheologiyot* 133, https://www.hadashot-esi.org.il/report_detail_eng.aspx?id=25951&mag_id=133 (last accessed May 2022).

Bron, H. (E.), 2022. 'Yafi'a' *Hadashot Arkheologiyot* 134, https://www.hadashot-esi.org.il/report_detail_eng.aspx?id=26111&mag_id=134 (last accessed May 2022).

Cohen, M., 2021. 'Yafi'a' *Hadashot Arkheologiyot* 133, https://www.hadashot-esi. org.il/report_detail_eng.aspx?id=25944&mag_id=133 (last accessed May 2022).

Sharvit, J., Makovsky, Y., Gatenio B., and Barkai, O., 2022. 'En Zippori', https://www. hadashot-esi.org.il/Report_Detail_Eng.aspx?id=26165 (last accessed May 2022).

Shemer, M., 2021. "Illut', *Hadashot Arkheologiyot* 133, https://www.hadashot-esi. org.il/report_detail_eng.aspx?id=26095&mag_id=133 (last accessed May 2022).

FURTHER READING

Aviam, M., 2004. *Jews, Pagans and Christians in the Galilee: 25 Years of Archaeological Excavations and Surveys: Hellenistic to Byzantine Periods*, Rochester University Press, Rochester, NY, and Woodbridge.

Fiensy, D. A., and Strange, J. R. (eds.), 2014–15 (2 volumes). *Galilee in the Late Second Temple and Mishnaic Periods, the Archaeological Record from Cities, Towns, and Villages*, Fortress Press, Minneapolis, MN.

Luff, R. M., 2019. *The Impact of Jesus in First-Century Palestine*, Cambridge University Press, Cambridge.

Magness, J., 2011. *Stone and Dung, Oil and Spit: Jewish Daily Life in the Time of Jesus*, Eerdmans, Grand Rapids, MI.

Ryan, J. J., 2021. *From the Passion to the Church of the Holy Sepulchre: Memories of Jesus in Place, Pilgrimage, and Early Holy Sites over the First Three Centuries*, Bloomsbury, London and New York.

Index

Note: Figures are indicated by an italic '*f*', following the page number.

(Excluding words in the book title and post-medieval personal names, and references to the Sisters of Nazareth site as a whole and the Cellar in general.)

For the benefit of digital users, indexed terms that span two pages (e.g., 52–53) may, on occasion, appear on only one of those pages.